Boundaries, Border Crossings, and Reinventing the Future

Conversation Pieces

A Small Paperback Series from Aqueduct Press
Subscriptions available: www.aqueductpress.com

1. The Grand Conversation
   Essays by L. Timmel Duchamp
2. With Her Body
   Short Fiction by Nicola Griffith
3. Changeling
   A Novella by Nancy Jane Moore
4. Counting on Wildflowers
   An Entanglement by Kim Antieau
5. The Traveling Tide
   Short Fiction by Rosaleen Love
6. The Adventures of the Faithful Counselor
   A Narrative Poem by Anne Sheldon
7. Ordinary People
   A Collection by Eleanor Arnason
8. Writing the Other
   A Practical Approach
   by Nisi Shawl & Cynthia Ward
9. Alien Bootlegger
   A Novella by Rebecca Ore
10. The Red Rose Rages (Bleeding)
    A Short Novel by L. Timmel Duchamp
11. Talking Back: Epistolary Fantasies
    edited by L. Timmel Duchamp
12. Absolute Uncertainty
    Short Fiction by Lucy Sussex
13. Candle in a Bottle
    A Novella by Carolyn Ives Gilman

14. Knots
    Short Fiction by Wendy Walker

15. Naomi Mitchison: A Profile of Her Life and Work
    A Monograph by Lesley A. Hall

16. We, Robots
    A Novella by Sue Lange

17. Making Love in Madrid
    A Novella by Kimberly Todd Wade

18. Of Love and Other Monsters
    A Novella by Vandana Singh

19. Aliens of the Heart
    Short Fiction by Carolyn Ives Gilman

20. Voices From Fairyland:
    The Fantastical Poems of Mary Coleridge, Charlotte Mew, and Sylvia Townsend Warner
    Edited and With Poems by Theodora Goss

21. My Death
    A Novella by Lisa Tuttle

22. De Secretis Mulierum
    A Novella by L. Timmel Duchamp

23. Distances
    A Novella by Vandana Singh

24. Three Observations and a Dialogue:
    Round and About SF
    Essays by Sylvia Kelso and a correspondence with Lois McMaster Bujold

25. The Buonarotti Quartet
    Short Fiction by Gwyneth Jones

26. Slightly Behind and to the Left
    Four Stories & Three Drabbles by Claire Light

27. Through the Drowsy Dark
    Short Fiction and Poetry by Rachel Swirsky

28. Shotgun Lullabies
    Stories and Poems by Sheree Renée Thomas

29. A Brood of Foxes
    A Novella by Kristin Livdahl
30. The Bone Spindle
    Poems and Short Fiction by Anne Sheldon
31. The Last Letter
    A Novella by Fiona Lehn
32. We Wuz Pushed
    On Joanna Russ and Radical Truth-Telling
    by Brit Mandelo
33. The Receptionist and Other Tales
    Poems by Lesley Wheeler
34. Birds and Birthdays
    Stories by Christopher Barzak
35. The Queen, the Cambion, and Seven Others
    Stories by Richard Bowes
36. Spring in Geneva
    A Novella by Sylvia Kelso
37. The XY Conspiracy
    A Novella by Lori Selke
38. Numa
    An Epic Poem
    by Katrinka Moore
39. Myths, Metaphors, and Science Fiction:
    Ancient Roots of the Literature of the Future
    Essays by Sheila Finch
40. NoFood
    Short Fiction by Sarah Tolmie
41. The Haunted Girl
    Poems and Short Stories by Lisa M. Bradley
42. Three Songs for Roxy
    A Novella by Caren Gussoff
43. Ghost Signs
    Poems and a Short Story by Sonya Taaffe

44. The Prince of the Aquamarines & The Invisible Prince: Two Fairy Tales
    by Louise Cavelier Levesque
45. Back, Belly, and Side: True Lies and False Tales
    Short Fiction by Celeste Rita Baker
46. A Day in Deep Freeze
    A Novella by Lisa Shapter
47. A Field Guide to the Spirits
    Poems by Jean LeBlanc
48. Marginalia to Stone Bird
    Poems by Rose Lemberg
49. Unpronounceable
    A Novella by Susan diRende
50. Sleeping Under the Tree of Life
    Poetry and Short Fiction by Sheree Renée Thomas
51. Other Places
    Short Fiction by Karen Heuler
52. Monteverde: Memoirs of an Interstellar Linguist
    A Novella by Lola Robles,
    translated by Lawrence Schimel
53. The Adventure of the Incognita Countess
    A Novella by Cynthia Ward
54. Boundaries, Border Crossings, and Reinventing the Future
    Essays and Short Fiction by Beth Plutchak
55. Liberating the Astronauts
    Poems by Christina Rau
56. In Search of Lost Time
    A Novella by Karen Heuler

About the Aqueduct Press Conversation Pieces Series

The feminist engaged with sf is passionately interested in challenging the way things are, passionately determined to understand how everything works. It is my constant sense of our feminist-sf present as a grand conversation that enables me to trace its existence into the past and from there see its trajectory extending into our future. A genealogy for feminist sf would not constitute a chart depicting direct lineages but would offer us an ever-shifting, fluid mosaic, the individual tiles of which we will probably only ever partially access. What could be more in the spirit of feminist sf than to conceptualize a genealogy that explicitly manifests our own communities across not only space but also time?

Aqueduct's small paperback series, Conversation Pieces, aims to both document and facilitate the "grand conversation." The Conversation Pieces series presents a wide variety of texts, including short fiction (which may not always be sf and may not necessarily even be feminist), essays, speeches, manifestoes, poetry, interviews, correspondence, and group discussions. Many of the texts are reprinted material, but some are new. The grand conversation reaches at least as far back as Mary Shelley and extends, in our speculations and visions, into the continually-created future. In Jonathan Goldberg's words, "To look forward to the history that will be, one must look at and retell the history that has been told." And that is what Conversation Pieces is all about.

L. Timmel Duchamp

Jonathan Goldberg, "The History That Will Be" in Louise Fradenburg and Carla Freccero, eds., *Premodern Sexualities* (New York and London: Routledge, 1996)

Conversation Pieces
Volume 54

Boundaries, Border Crossings, and Reinventing the Future

by
Beth Plutchak

Published by Aqueduct Press
PO Box 95787
Seattle, WA 98145-2787
www.aqueductpress.com

ISBN: 978-1-61976-121-6

Cover photo © 1975 by Beth Plutchak:
Original Block Print of Mary Shelley by Justin Kempton:
www.writersmugs.com

Prior Publication Acknowledgments:

"The Alien Among Us," WisCon 21 Souvenir Book, ed. Beth Plutchak, WisCon and SF3 (the Society for the Furtherance and Study of Fantasy and Science Fiction), May 1997.

"Sheri Tepper is My Hero," WisCon 22 Souvenir Book, ed. Beth Plutchak, WisCon and SF3 (the Society for the Furtherance and Study of Fantasy and Science Fiction), May 1998.

"Challenging the Narrative of the Undeserving Poor," *WisCon Chronicles Vol 7 Shattering Ableist Narratives*, ed. JoSelle Vanderhooft, Aqueduct Press, 2013.

"Is WisCon Feminist?" *WisCon Chronicles Vol. 8 Re-Generating WisCon*, ed. Rebecca J. Holden, Aqueduct Press, 2014

For M, J, and W

Contents

Is WisCon Feminist?

> At WisCon 37 in 2013 I took part in a panel titled "Is WisCon Feminist?" with this description: Is WisCon really a Feminist Science Fiction Convention? Is feminism narrowly defined as women's interests and women's power, or has feminism itself changed to include all forms of social and political activism? Would it be closer to reality to call WisCon the Leading Activist Science Fiction Convention? My co-panelists were Ian K. Hagemann (moderator), Jennie Devereaux-Weber, Jeanne Gomoll, and Piglet. The following essay was inspired by this panel and by my own long and often uncomfortable relationship with feminism, both intersectional and not.

Did I ever tell you about that time I got kicked out of Second Wave Feminism? Well, I didn't get a severance letter or anything, but I felt unwelcomed nonetheless, and in all the years since I've never felt welcomed back. You wouldn't know it by looking at me, of course. I'm sixty years old, white, cis-gendered, apparently able-bodied and straight. But, I never fit in with the goals of white middle-class feminism. I'm like that guy in the TV show *Life* who said, "I don't not say the things other people don't say." For instance, why do we call it Second Wave Feminism? That only makes sense if we start counting with the assumption that no one in the wide world ever thought of women's powerlessness in society until a bunch of white women decided they wanted the vote in the late nineteenth century.

But I digress (I learned that word in college). This is the story of how intersectionality saved my life, of how the women who occupied spaces I didn't belong to were willing to have my back when I needed them. And, by the way, when I say saved my life, I don't mean metaphorically. I know the difference between a metaphorical argument and a literal one. Literally, the does-it-count-as-abuse-if-he-hits-you-in-an-alcoholic-blackout-and-can't-remember-it kind of saving my life.

You know by now that I came of age in the radical sixties. Change not only seemed possible; it seemed inevitable. When you are young and going through a thing for the first time, it seems like the first time for the whole wide world. That's what it was like in 1970. We had the power to ask questions that had never been asked before and to put the answers together in totally new ways. And power was shifting—we felt it; we were often the cause of it. We'd counted our years by the deaths of our leaders: Kennedy and Shabazz and King and another Kennedy. It was a horrible time, but it was a time of hope and possibility.

I was active in the Student Mobilization Committee to End the War in Vietnam in college. I'd grown up hearing stories of the Freedom Riders and Malcolm X and Martin Luther King Jr. Civil Rights was the important struggle of our time. Opposition to American Imperialism in Viet Nam was the logical outgrowth of that struggle and accessible to a working-class white girl, especially one who got to go to college.

My cousin was the one who convinced me I needed to attend a consciousness-raising session. I wasn't opposed to the idea; it just didn't seem that important in the greater scheme of things, you know. Our analysis consisted of finding the thing that's the worst, solve the oppression that is the last thing the oppressors are willing to give up. Once you unravel that thing, the rest of it has to fall apart. We weren't aware that sometimes things need to be ripped apart at the seams.

We spent a lot of time arguing over which was the worst evil, Sexism or Capitalism. We didn't even have the word intersectionality at the time. We were overly simplistic, to be sure. John Lennon and Yoko Ono held bed-ins, and Lennon began singing "Woman is the N***r of the World." The National Organization for Women loved it. Any more complicated thoughts that Ono might have had on racism and sexism never made it to the six o'clock news. Audre Lorde didn't write her letter to Mary Daly until 1980. It surprises me now to still hear people arguing which is the worst oppression, or counting them up, as if who has the most wins, or if one by one they negate your privileges. This is how those in power tore us apart in the first place. (I think we ought to own up to that much at least.) This is how the powers that be set up tactical gains that could be easily dismantled.

The sad thing, looking back, is that we didn't even understand where *we* were coming from. We were working-class kids, raised in paper-mill towns. We'd been taught by school and church and family to believe that life was ordered, organized, and that "the way things worked" was discoverable.

Those who knew what that was certainly could and did use that knowledge against the less powerful, but we thought life had rules, you could choose to break them, but the rules were what they were. Most of us were the first generation in our families to attend college (never mind that we were girls). Feminism's goal of equal pay for equal work and equal opportunity resonated. None of us wanted to grow up to marry the boy who worked at the mill. We wanted our own independence.

In a country that denies the existence of class, we had no idea that class issues were at play. We had no idea that other white women wanted access to what *their* men had, the running and the ownership of the mill, the factory, the whatever. We thought we'd been invited to join *their* club. So we turned our backs on the women who were really our natural allies.

We were woefully unprepared for how easily we could be manipulated by the systems and processes that had formed us, that were like breathing to us, and that we had purposely been culturally blinkered to.

That whole white-is-the-default-human thing, for instance. While white women sat in consciousness-raising circles talking about how men weren't the default human, we were totally prepared to claim that privileged default position for ourselves without a second's reflection. We had heated arguments at my almost totally white, northern Wisconsin college about whether to do outreach to the few black women who sat in the back rows in our classes. But, would they be willing to choose feminism over race? Would they be willing to admit how sexist the Black Panthers were? You know, Stokely Carmichael. *We* argued that, while none of *them* were even present.

Was I a part of these indignities? Of course I was. I didn't know how to stop them or process them, really. I lived in a very insular, very homophobic, very white space. Micro-aggressions were what they were. I can understand that now, how little by little things chip away at you, until you can't even see the damage done.

There were positive things that came out of those sessions, though. Here is a thing I will never forget. I was still more involved in the anti-war movement than in the feminist movement, but by 1970-71 most of the anti-war conventions I went to had a feminist track. An absolutely amazing, to me, thing happened at one of these. I went to a session on women's issues. There were one or two men in the room. The leader of the session asked if it was alright with everyone for the men to stay. She asked for a show of hands. There was only one woman who objected, so I figured majority rules, but that wasn't how it worked. The men were asked to leave because one woman was uncomfortable, because one woman felt she would not be able to participate fully if there were men in the room. It was the first time I'd ever encountered that kind of concept. That the most vulnerable could have the most say over issues that directly affected them. (WisCon had an opportunity to recreate this in 1999 with people of color, but it took us ten years to get our act together.) The seventies were heady times anyway, and that is the feeling that people remember with nostalgia. We were ending the war in Viet Nam. We were going to legalize abortion and pass the Equal Rights Amendment. We were also discovering our sexuality for the first time. Some of my friends were on the pill. Am I the only woman my age who remembers the summer of love? Young women nowadays seem to think we were all prudes.

And now, as a country we seem to have forgotten all of it. All the baby boomers on TV are white and middle class and successful, oh and liberal and artistic and in charge. When I sit around with women my age who were feminists way back when, predominantly white women, because I still live in predominantly white spaces, they tend to bemoan the old days. As though, if the kids just got it, got what we'd accomplished, if the kids knew how relevant it still was to their lives, then we could go forward and make change happen again. We want it to be a continuum, and we want it to succeed before we die.

But, I always feel that what we really owe these young women is an apology; I think we need to tell them that if feminism seems irrelevant to their concerns, it's not because it is irrelevant, it's because we lost. We made compromises to achieve narrow goals; we threw our sisters of color under the bus. We convinced ourselves we weren't like poor white women. We asked poor women and all women of color to wait. We wouldn't ask for full reproductive rights; let's get abortion and birth control first, we said. We wouldn't ask for a restructuring of corporate capitalism we'd just be satisfied with equal pay and equal access for now. We wanted the ERA, equality with the boys, even though what the boys had varied wildly by race and class. We weren't brave enough to think that through, not to mention the white women who never wanted to anyway, thank you very much.

Why do you think the same battles are being fought all over again? It's not entirely our fault. We were played. But, we have to recognize that and own our part in it.

Anyway, that was all a long time ago. By the time I was nineteen I was pregnant (I remember the summer of love) and on my way to Alaska to live in the woods. I chose dropping out and starting fresh, rather than changing society from within. But, that wasn't the part that made my white feminist friends uncomfortable around me. The part they didn't like was that I was a walking example that even if we got access to birth control, it wasn't foolproof. And to make matters worse, I wanted that baby. They needed to "other" me. They needed to "other" me fast.

I read a lot of theory during my Alaska years, but I never was a part of a feminist movement after that. I could no longer pass as an acceptable feminist you see, even less so when I came back to Wisconsin both poor and a survivor. Once you've been put in the victim box, you need saving. Your agency is gone unless you deny your membership in marginalized groups. Even at WisCon I made people uncomfortable when I refused to fit my assigned narrative.

The women I hung out with in Alaska weren't activists; they were other women just trying to get by. And for the first time, I was living in a culturally diverse community. Class and gender united us. We were trying to survive poverty and violence and alcoholism. Getting by meant surviving another day.

Okay, here's the part of the story where I keep getting stuck—trying to write some kind of a transition from the part where I give you my early experiences with anti-war and feminist movements, my increasing awareness of the links between racism, classism, and sexism, to where I end up in Alaska married to a violent alcoholic, with three kids, and so poor we didn't "have a pot to piss in," as we used to say.

You see, it's always the same when I tell this story. You judge me, to see where I went wrong, what mistakes I made that turned me into a victim. I understand that you need it to be on me, that you need to believe that anyone can read the signs. That there is a way to tell who will become violent and that those of us who don't see it are willfully blinkered, or self-destructive, or just plain stupid (which doesn't mean intellectually impaired; it means ignorant through virtue of culture, race, and/or class, just to be clear). And I know that you don't mean to say it was my fault or that I deserved it. I know that because you told me so, you told me exactly that—word for word, when I reacted to what I perceived as condemnation of *my* choices and *my* actions. I realize that the reason you need it to be me, not him, not society, not systemic, is for you to feel safe, for you to feel that you have boundaries that cannot be breached. But, you are wrong.

You ask me, "Why didn't I leave?" As though that is the final nail in the coffin, the final proof that it was on me, even though I left over thirty years ago, I moved four thousand miles away, and he's been dead for five years. You ask me, "Why didn't you leave—sooner?"

I can't protect you. I can't even talk to you anymore.

So, I'm going to talk to someone else. Because you are there too. Oh, I can see you standing there, practicing invisibility. I know how dangerous it is to be noticed. I recognize you. I've been you, and it's you I really need to talk to, because I know how to get out alive.

There's an old joke that they tell at AA meetings. A guy falls down a manhole and he can't get out. He tries everything, but he's stuck. He calls out to passersby to help him, but they keep right on walking. And then, finally, finally, somebody stops. And he yells up at him, "Can you help me? I'm stuck down here." And the other guy says, "Sure." And he jumps right down the manhole. And the first guy says, "What's the matter with you? Now we're both stuck down here." And the second guy says, "No, it's okay. I've been down here before, and I know the way out."

Yeah, yeah, yeah, I know you don't think you deserve anything yet, but we worked that out in Al-Anon, and I'm going to tell you how.

There is a list that floats around telling us how to recognize a potential abuser, and that list always leaves so much out. It always leaves out that he is charming, considerate, the kindest person you have ever met. That initially, he puts your needs first, always. When you are with friends, he is the first one to have your back, and he has a lot of friends. He is fun to be around and includes you in everything. He brings you out of yourself and makes you feel valuable in a way no one else has ever done. And when you first start to see his demons, you want to help him, protect him, look out for him, as he does for you.

And when things start to go bad, it is always little things, inconsequential things, and you start to mistrust your own judgment. He stayed out too late with friends, and are you making too much of it? He spent all the money you had set aside for groceries, but maybe he did spend it on parts for the car, but the car still isn't running, and you'd better not stress him out with your doubts or he'll never get it fixed.

Human beings are resilient, you know, and things get bad one little thing at a time, so we learn to cope. And we start to mistrust our own perceptions of what is really going on.

Batterers will isolate you, but it's hard to recognize that. At first you are happy, because you want to spend more time at home. You want to be a family and stop bar-hopping and hanging out. You realize you don't like his friends anyway, and you never really made friends that were yours, so spending less time with them isn't a sacrifice.

You go to work wearing a mask, another form of invisibility. You want to appear to be the happy family you thought you were going to be, and you can't appear to be too different, because then your co-workers will be suspicious of you. You need to focus on your job and get the job done. You need the money.

So there is a separation between the real world, the world out there, and the world you sink into at home, which is less real somehow, because nobody would believe you if they knew how it really was, and they would start to judge you, and you can't trust your own perceptions anyway. How could you? The person you should most be able to trust in the world, your partner, the father of your children, is untrustworthy. And you picked him, so your judgment is equally suspect.

So there I was in Alaska. Not at all what I'd thought it would be. Early on we stayed at my husband's aunt's house, and he went to work in construction. In Anchorage, not "the woods" at all. The first time he hit me, I was totally taken aback, and he was so, so sorry. He promised he would never do it again. And you know what? He never did. That was our line in the sand, as long as he never hit me, I had to stay. Whatever else happened, I had to figure out how to cope with it, and I did, giving up parts of myself bit by bit, too slowly to notice how much I'd lost. Micro-aggressions.

The last few years we were together he threatened to kill me on a daily basis. He put his fist through the cupboard door near where I was standing, through the drywall above the bed while I was lying there. Just to show me he was strong enough to break me. He told me I was lucky because I'd have driven anybody else to hurt me by now, and he had refrained. I know to some of you that sounds horrible, but you know, I had no way to judge if that were true, and remember, the message I got over and over again was that if I was a victim, it was my fault. So, I know people hate hearing this, but with the best of intentions they are also complicit.

Anyway, I did what I always did when I needed to figure stuff out. I read. I read science fiction: *Of Mist and Grass and Sand*, by Vonda McIntyre; *Women of Wonder*, edited by Pamela Sargent; everything by Ursula K. Le Guin and Cordwainer Smith and James Tiptree Jr.; so much post-apocalyptic stuff. It's funny how when you are living in the middle of an apocalypse, post-apocalyptic seems hopeful.

I read nonfiction, too. The women's movement of the popular press at the time was Gloria Steinem and Betty Friedan. Betty Friedan wrote a new book. The gist of it was that feminism was also good for men. That if we wanted to make feminist gains we needed to embrace the men, stop making them feel so threatened. Stop talking about what we wanted, and talk about what they had to gain. Honestly, I'd spent my life trying to give him what was best for him, and it wasn't working out too well.

The only people who were ever honest with me about what I was going through were the lesbian separatists I met at a Klondyke Chorus concert. I made two friends in particular who introduced me to a feminist analysis, right when I needed it by the way, that was pro-family while questioning so-called "traditional" families. They encouraged me to be brave enough to put myself and my children first. Not that I was accepted by everybody there either. I had a son. I spent a deal of time with my two friends who were planning a child. What if their child were a boy? Would their community still accept them? They needed my experiences as the mother of a son, while they worked through changes to their own feminist analysis.

I found my way to Al-Anon eventually; I don't remember how, but I do remember that I thought it would encourage him to go to AA. I thought our problem was his drinking, and if he gave up the alcohol he could cope. I went to Al-Anon, because I thought it was a way I could help him. Lots of people do.

I didn't take it well, at first, when I found out it was supposed to be about me, and about finding my way to what I wanted. That kind of thinking (what *I* wanted?) didn't even make any sense to me anymore. And I was so grounded in stereotypes about why I'd ended up where I was that I brought all that self-hate and all those stereotypes with me.

I brought other stereotypes as well. I thought that if the Chicana who came to our meetings just wouldn't be so loud, or so angry, her husband wouldn't hit her so much. Or if she didn't fight back, why the hell did she fight back? I wondered. She was going to get herself killed.

Somebody had to sit me down and walk me through it; how it wasn't her fault, and it wasn't her culture; it was just her, trying to get by, trying to figure out a way to live.

I thought that the Native Woman in our group would be able to escape with her kids and get off welfare if she'd just get a job. I thought that until I ran into her one day at the local diner, where she worked full-time but earned so little money she still qualified for assistance. I found out that she was working with her sponsor to find a way to tell her husband that he couldn't come back, and keep herself safe, and keep her kids safe, and not lose her home, and not lose her job.

So, the world wasn't just starting to look different for me. Other people's stories were changing me as well. I told you I was going to tell you how I got out. We made a bargain with each other, you see. The bargain was beautiful in its simplicity. It shouldn't have worked, but it did.

I couldn't believe in myself. I couldn't see beyond my shame and my complicity. I knew I didn't deserve anything better, but Al-Anon told me, that's okay. You don't have to believe in you. We know how impossible that is, so we'll believe in you for you. I can't even begin to tell you how empowering that was.

Other people tell you, you need to love yourself, but what you really need is for someone to love you unconditionally when you know you are unlovable. What you really need is for someone to believe the story of your life, your story, the way you tell it, the way you've experienced it. You begin to deserve to live, when someone outside yourself believes the story of your life and believes it has value and believes you have value in it.

I was different after that. I didn't practice invisibility everywhere I went. At work I didn't talk about my reality, but I didn't hide it either.

So, that was the bargain. You believe in me, and I believe in you. That's the bargain that keeps people living on the margins alive. That is the story of how I survived, but it's also a bigger story than that. I'm going to get back to WisCon in a minute, because that's where we grow this into the story of how we are going to change the world.

My best friend at work during the Alaska years was a black woman, with narrow hips and wide shoulders and short red hair. She was outgoing and had a kind word for everybody, but she didn't pull any punches, either. People knew what she thought about a thing.

But, there was a thing we didn't talk about, not until we knew each other really well, and not unless we were in the break room alone together, where we couldn't be overheard, and that was—living with an abusive alcoholic husband. Sarah was very open with advice for white people, about why black people did what they did, about growing up in the segregated south in a sharecropper family on a pecan farm. She wasn't a feminist or a black activist, she was just someone getting by who liked to tell stories.

But through her stories, she was also engaged in reframing the way the world looked at her. She had no interest in becoming another black woman victimized by a black man. That was a tired old story, and it wasn't going to be her story. She had no black feminist analysis for what she was going through. bell hooks didn't write *Ain't I a Woman?: Black Women and Feminism* until 1981. Anyway, analysis is a luxury when you are trying to stay alive until tomorrow.

We tested each other out slowly at first, her telling me about the time her husband chased her boyfriend out of the house with a gun, and she told him she didn't want him to wave a gun around in the house in front of their girls. And he told her didn't she feel bad then, that he'd had to come to the house and do it? "Uh huh," I said. "He twisted that back on you. He was wrong."

I asked her, "Is somebody responsible if he hits you while he's in a blackout and can't remember that he did?" She said, "If he did it, he did it. He's responsible."

These aren't the kind of stories you can share with just anybody. These stories freak normal people out, and then they have you questioning yourself. And honestly, when you're in those situations, it's just not safe to keep second-guessing yourself. So, even though Sarah wasn't in Al-Anon, we kept the bargain with each other anyway. I believed her stories and she believed mine. And not just our retelling of our experiences, although that was a big thing in and of itself, but our reactions to those experiences, our interpretations. Those were just as important.

She invited me to her house to meet her friends. I was her only white friend. And I began to see that she had a double kind of invisibility, the invisibility she wore around people who would blame her for the violence in her home and another invisibility that she wore when she was in a space that was predominantly white people.

Sarah and I went through our divorces together, and even though I haven't seen her in years, I owe her my life (again, not metaphorical). Because in the end I did leave. I left him. I left my job. I left Alaska. I started over again in Wisconsin.

⚬

My first WisCon was WisCon Twenty. Ursula K. Le Guin was the guest of honor. Pamela Sargent was just, you know, there. I can't say I found my home, or my "tribe," like some people do when they discover WisCon. But, I discovered a place where two things were important: story as a vehicle to change the world and reaching beyond a white, middle-class definition of feminism.

Anyway, that's the long-form version of how I ended up on the "Is WisCon Feminist?" panel. That's a pretty long explanation for introductions, so I think I said something like "I have been interested in questions of feminism and intersectionality for a long time."

We were all in agreement that feminism isn't feminism if it isn't intersectional, so that part of the panel went pretty smoothly. We all had either attended WisCon for a long time, or spent many years on the ConCom, or both. And Jeanne Gomoll was there, and we wouldn't even have a WisCon without her. And even though I hadn't been there since the beginning, I'd spent enough years on the ConCom to witness many of the behind-the-scenes fights for the soul of WisCon, so to speak. So there was a little bit of nostalgic reminiscing, too.

And this led to a discussion of how WisCon had grown and spawned all the other organizations that grew out of it, Tiptree and Carl Brandon and Broad Universe, the sister organizations. We were building a narrative, you see. A narrative about all the good WisCon had done. And about how it mattered that that good was intersectional. How feminism wasn't just for white women.

But, this narrative was starting to go wrong for me, because we were glossing over the disagreements and the struggles that had really happened in order for the narrative to function smoothly. But remember, I believe that people's lives depend upon the true stories being told. That's part of the bargain.

It was Ian Hagemann, if I remember correctly, who brought up that Carl Brandon wasn't so much born of WisCon as born out of frustration *with* WisCon. It was 1999, the year the ConCom had promised a safe space for people of color, a space modeled on the feminist track at that anti-war rally I told you about at the beginning of this piece.

At the last minute this space was taken away and explicitly made open to anyone, with no explanation, just a last minute change. So the people of color, some of whom were only there on scholarship or they wouldn't have been able to attend at all, met anyway. And met alone, without the sanction of the convention, to talk about their anger, and hurt, and disappointment. Carl Brandon was founded at that convention, but it was not a painless birth.

So in that moment I decided I needed to tell the story the way I remembered it. I decided that people needed to know what really happened, but I was a little nervous about bringing it up, because Jeanne was on the panel, and she was at that meeting, and I'm still not sure why the real story never did come out.

I remember that ConCom meeting very well, where the safe space fell apart. We were at the Concourse, sitting around tables set up to form a square. Jeanne was Programming Chair that year, and the other half of Programming was on the phone. I think it was Debbie Notkin. We'd just been going around in a circle, giving our progress reports.

This was one of the late meetings. We were getting really close to the convention. I didn't have anything to report. I'd edited the Souvenir Book again that year, and the Souvenir Book and Pocket Program had already gone to the printer.

So, Jeanne and Debbie gave their report, and nobody really paid much attention, because we were all thinking about the things we were trying to finalize, but part of the process at this time was to compare notes with the hotel liaison, to talk about which program items might need the bigger rooms and which might need special rooms. And then Jeanne mentioned that they'd also need special signage for the safe space, so that people would know that it had been set aside for the sole use of people of color.

One of the men in the room said, "I don't think I heard that right. You can't have a space that everybody who's purchased a membership isn't welcome in." He wasn't agitated, yet.

This was something that'd been in the works for six months or more. Jeanne and a few of the other ConCom members tried to explain to him the reasoning behind it and why it was important, and he went ballistic.

He jumped out of his chair and towered over one of the women sitting in the room, shaking his fists at her.

Now this was something I recognized, because he didn't pick Jeanne, who was the Programming Chair, he didn't pick the last person to say a thing, he picked a woman who was shy and retiring and had her reasons for wanting to avoid confrontation, and decided to physically intimidate her, to make his point. The rest of the room froze. Wisconsin niceness didn't believe what we were seeing and didn't know what to do.

My hands were shaking because I didn't know how out of hand this was going to get, but I had my secret weapon, which was, whatever he was going to do, I knew I could survive worse, because you know, I already had. So I told him we were not going to back down. That this needed to happen. And we didn't cave as a group under threat of violence in the moment, which was something. But, we did cave later out of fear.

Some of the other guys in the room got up and got him to sit back down, and by then the room was divided, because people thought there were reasonable arguments to be made about whether the ConCom could keep Programming's promise. And the first guy kept insisting they couldn't do it and finally said that if they went through with it, he was going to sue the ConCom and everyone on it, and if that destroyed WisCon, so be it. And I'm not using his name on purpose, because it doesn't matter. He was just *that* guy. There's always somebody willing to be that guy.

Somebody on the ConCom consulted a lawyer who told them, that yes he could sue. Even though this is America and anybody can sue anybody for anything, in the end there weren't enough people on the ConCom who could get past the threat of a lawsuit that might bankrupt WisCon. They decided to come up with a compromise. I didn't agree. I still don't. I lost that fight.

At the panel, Jeanne seemed a little bit relieved that it was out in the open. And she added to it a little from her perspective and pointed out that eventually we did get there and provided the space (not coincidentally, I think, until after we got a lawyer on the ConCom and purchased event insurance and liability insurance for the SF3 Board).

Ian told me later that he'd gotten into Madison the night before the convention opened that year, in time to help with packet stuffing, and the first thing they had him do was to put stickers on the program book covering up the notice that the space set aside for people of color was for people of color only, because you know it wasn't anymore.

I don't tell this story to make a point that everything turned out all right in the end. Because it isn't the end, yet. And the journey is not a smooth transition. Every step is a fight. And for me, at least, it's harder to keep fighting if I don't own up to all the parts of the struggle, the good and the bad, and the parts that people don't like to talk about because somebody will disapprove. This is why I still can't play the game the good, white, feminists of WisCon play, the reminiscing game. This is what goes through my head when the wistful reminiscing of the good old days gone by starts, "Oh, don't give up on me now; there is work to be done. We lost. Own it. Change the future."

This is why intersectionality in fandom matters, why people of color in fandom are *important.* And I get it; you've been telling us this at least as long as I've been alive, and we are very poor listeners. I know you are putting it all on the line just by showing up. You are in fandom because *you* need *your* story told—the story about people of color or disabled people or trans people or poor women or any other story that isn't being told—but, I'm here because *I* need your story. That's the bargain. I believe in you even though I am steeped in institutional racism, because somewhere down the line someone like you believed in me. It doesn't matter if traditional publishing doesn't get your work or want your work; there are alternatives now. Find the small presses; self-publish; I need your books.

Honestly, it doesn't even matter if you don't know anything about the bargain. You don't need to keep it for my sake. I survived. I don't need it anymore. I had it when I did. But, I'll keep my part of the bargain. And I'll keep it not because it's fair, not because it's the right thing to do, or the feminist thing to do, but because your stories will continue to save lives. Stories have the power to change the world. As long as your story is real, so is mine, and the fact that yours exists kept me alive and keeps me alive. How could I ever forget a thing like that?

Notes

The term intersectionality was coined by Dr. Kimberlé Williams Crenshaw, professor at UCLA School of Law and Columbia Law School, specializing in race and gender issues. She coined the term to address the way the law responded to issues where both race and gender discrimination were involved. In Social Justice Theory the term has expanded to cover whenever multiple forms of systemic oppression are at play. These are referred to as "axes of oppression."

One of the pitfalls for individuals who only experience one axis of oppression (such as a white, straight, cisgendered, able-bodied, middle-class woman) is assuming that intersectionality is a sum game—that oppressions are added up as an individual moves further from the societal "norm" of straight, white, male. This outlook minimizes the specific dangers of living at multiple axes of oppression. For example, black women do not experience the oppression of white women *plus* the oppression of black men, but experience unique oppression based upon stereotypes surrounding black female sexuality, stereotypes that arose during slavery to justify the rape of black women.

The term **micro-aggression** was coined by Dr. Chester Middlebrook Pierce, Emeritus Professor of Education and Psychiatry at Harvard Medical School. According to Pierce (via Wikipedia), "the chief vehicles (sic) for proracist behaviors are micro-aggressions. These are subtle, stunning, often automatic, and nonverbal exchanges which are 'put-downs' of blacks by offenders."

For example, while taking my daily bus ride we often stopped to pick up a small group of young black men. The bus was filled with white middle-class individuals going home from work. As the young men boarded the bus, the white people shifted uncomfortably in their seats, some of them moving belongings so that none of the young men would sit next to them. This behavior seems minor and innocuous to those perpetrating it, particularly since it is an auto response rather than something done with intent. The impact on the young men is not so subtle. Their demeanor visibly changed from high school kids, laughing and goofing off at the bus stop, to very guarded body language and blank facial expressions as they boarded the bus and looked for seats. These young men were reminded every time they boarded public transportation that white America sees them as dangerous.

For anyone in a marginalized group, micro-aggressions are both experienced frequently and denied as either not happening at all or as having no real meaning by those not experiencing them.

⟜

I can't remember when I first saw the ubiquitous **list** of "how to recognize a potential abuser." In researching this article I googled the term and came up with 5,640,000 results. Present day lists are still widely disseminated by domestic violence and women's health organizations. The language surrounding the current lists does not blame the victim as overtly as was common in the 1970s and 1980s; however, they still rely on the assumption that women can escape battery if they know enough to recognize that they are in danger and if they get out in time.

Blaming the victim is a defense mechanism against an unjust world. If the victim is totally blameless, that disrupts the notion that the world is a safe place and that a person is protected from bad things by proper and knowable behaviors. While I was working on this article a link to one of these lists showed up on my Tumblr feed, and another one showed up on my Facebook feed, posted by a well-meaning acquaintance who had no knowledge of my history as a domestic violence survivor.

Sources

Anonymous. *Courage to Change: One Day at a Time in Al-Anon* (referred to in Al-Anon as the little blue book). Virginia Beach, VA: Al-Anon Family Group Headquarters.

Crenshaw, Dr. Kimberlé Williams. "Intersectionality the Double Bind of Race and Gender," 2004, *Perspectives* http://www.americanbar.org/content/dam/aba/publishing/perspectives_magazine/women_perspectives_Spring2004CrenshawPSP.authcheckdam.pdf.

Eisenstein, Zilla R., editor. *Capitalist Patriarchy and the Case for Socialist Feminism.* New York: Monthly Review Press, 1979.

Friedan, Betty. *The Second Stage*, October. New York: Simon and Schuster, 1981.

hooks, bell. *Ain't I a Woman, black women and feminism.* Boston: South End Press, 1981.

hooks, bell and Melissa Harris Perry. "Black Female Voices: A Public Dialogue Between bell hooks and Melissa Harris Perry" (VIDEO), November 11, 2013, The New School, http://www.youtube.com/watch?v=5OmgqXao1ng.

Hull, Gloria T., Patricia Bell Scott, and Barbara Smith, editors. *But Some of Us Are Brave.* New York: *All The Women Are White and All the Blacks are Men.* The Feminist Press at CUNY, 1982.

Kendall, Mikki. #solidarityisforwhitewomen, 2013. http://storify.com/niche/solidarity-is-for-white-women.

"#SolidarityIsForWhiteWomen Creator, Mikki Kendal, Speaks About Women Of Color," Feminism (VIDEO), 2013, Huffington Post, http://www.huffingtonpost.com/2013/08/13/solidarityisforwhitewomen-creator-mikki-kendal-women-of-color-feminism-_n_3749589.html.

Lorde, Audre. *Sister Outsider: Essays and Speeches.* Freedom, CA: Crossing Press, Crossing Press Feminist Series, 1984. The text of the letter first made public in 1979 is available here: http://www.historyisaweapon.com/defcon1/lordeopenlettertomarydaly.html.

Moraga, Cherríe and Gloria Anzaldúa. *This Bridge Called My Back, Writings by Radical Women of Color.* Watertown, MA: Persephone Press, 1981.

Steiner, Leslie Morgan. "Why Domestic Violence Victims Don't Leave" (VIDEO), November 2012, TEDx. http://www.ted.com/talks/leslie_morgan_steiner_why_domestic_violence_victims_don_t_leave.html.

Challenging the Narrative of the Undeserving Poor

We want to help the poor, I suppose, but we don't want to help people who don't deserve it, people who won't help themselves. But, how do we know who is and isn't deserving? Who controls that narrative? Let's unwind this a little bit, shall we?

Background

In 1962, Michael Harrington's book *The Other America* was published. At the time the United States was in a period of economic expansion, and Harrington's purpose was to expose poverty in the United States that was largely invisible and unaffected by the increasing prosperity of the many. At the time, the rate of poverty was eleven percent.

In response to the book, President Kennedy introduced the War on Poverty. Social safety-net measures, which had been introduced under Roosevelt, were expanded, and new ones introduced. After Kennedy's assassination, Johnson continued the War on Poverty and made it a cornerstone of his presidency.

In the mid-seventies, class mobility declined, and the amount of wealth and income going to those at the top of the economic ladder started to increase exponentially. Economically we were in a period of increasing inflation and stagnating wage growth, a condition that economists had considered impossible.

Ever-improving quality of life, considered the birthright of the Baby Boomers, had been realized through ever-increasing productivity gains in post-industrial America—income gains that were largely funded through increased productivity. The historical relation of productivity to hourly compensation is illustrated here:

Disconnect between productivity and a typical workers compensation, 1948-2015

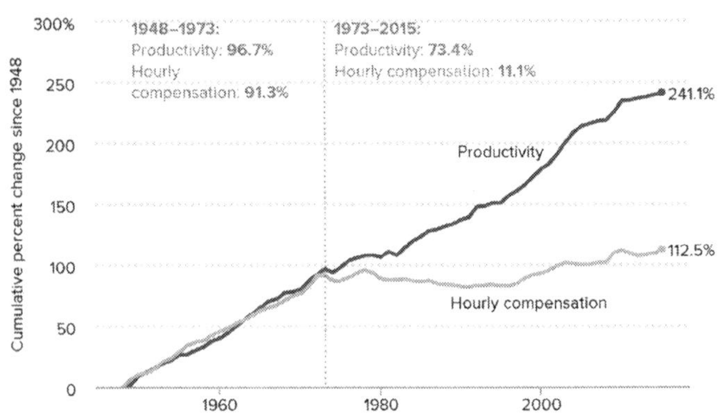

Note: Data are for average hourly compensation of production/nonsupervisory workers in the private sector and net productivity of the total economy. "Net productivity" is the growth of output of goods and services minus depreciation per hour worked.

Source: EPI analysis of data from the BEA and BLS (see technical appendix of *Understanding the Historic Divergence Between Productivity and a Typical Worker's Pay* for more detailed information)

Economic Policy Institute

As workers lost political and bargaining power in an era of high unemployment, the connection between productivity growth and income growth was severed. Every recession since the mid-seventies has been followed by a so-called "jobless recovery" and stagnant wage growth. After 1973, productivity continued to grow at record rates. The economy could have afforded to increase pay, but politics and the popular narrative had changed.

In 1981 Ronald Reagan broke the Air Traffic Controllers Union. This was a pivotal event in what had been a slow decline in the perceived relevance of unions to the majority of working Americans.

In 1984 Charles Murray's book *Losing Ground* was published. His analysis of what was wrong with the "Welfare State" was driven by a belief that the poor are poor because they make the wrong moral choices, and that the purpose of policy should not be to alleviate poverty, but to change behavior. This was not the first or last time that poverty was tied to the morality of the poor.

In 1996 under a supposedly left-leaning President Clinton, "welfare reform" was accomplished through the passage of the revealingly named "Personal Responsibility and Work Opportunity Reconciliation Act of 1996." This law has proven long on personal responsibility and short on opportunity.

As I write this in the fall of 2012, census data has just been released giving a US poverty rate of fifteen percent from the most currently available data.

All of the above events are interconnected and depend upon a popular narrative that leads the majority of the voting public to believe that the right policy choices are being made. In particular, people believe popular narratives that make undermining the social safety net, further impoverishing the poor, and virtually unattainable class mobility acceptable. People who may be only one paycheck or one illness away from poverty themselves support programs they believe are ultimately in their own best interest, because they believe in a particular narrative of the undeserving poor.

People are inclined to believe culturally predominant narratives even when they contradict their own lived experiences. The famous Alaskan artist and writer Joe Senungetuk tells a story of learning about Eskimos as a schoolboy. He received his textbook and read to his surprise that Eskimos lived in igloos. Since he had never lived in an igloo, since no one in his family had ever lived in an igloo, since he'd never known anyone who lived in an igloo, he thought they must be talking about Canadian Eskimos.

The Myth of the Undeserving Poor

I became a member of the undeserving poor through marriage and alcoholism. My family fits very neatly into the narrative of the undeserving poor. I know what people think. Most people are unaware of the links between alcoholism and untreated mental illness, specifically the urge to self-medicate when treatment is non-existent or unavailable. I certainly was unaware when I married.

There are many ways we as a society determine who of the poor are and are not deserving. Many of these definitions are dependent upon racist stereotypes, such as a belief that members of minority groups are lazy or overly self-indulgent. Others are dependent upon deep misunderstandings of the nature of addiction and mental illness. The story we tell about the undeserving poor is framed by the idea that they make choices that cause their poverty, choices upstanding citizens would not make. This narrative is extremely useful in providing absolution of any responsibility for each other, useful in protecting us from any charge of culpability in supporting institutions that make escape from poverty virtually impossible.

I know what people think when they hear my story. They think that alcoholism is a choice, and if they see a connection to mental illness, the associated fear and stigma makes it even more unacceptable.

My husband's alcoholism was complicated by depression, cognitive disability, and childhood trauma. When his behavior endangered me and endangered my children, I was ashamed. This was in keeping with the narrative, a narrative I believed. A narrative that told me that everyone has complete free choice in everything, and that compulsive, addictive behavior is a chosen behavior. There is additional stigma attached to asking for help. If, as the narrative tells us, poverty is simply an outcome of poor choices and lack of willpower, asking for help in and of itself marks you as a lesser person.

Health insurance and healthcare policies in the United States marginalize people with invisible disabilities. While people who are mentally ill and self-medicating with drugs and alcohol are indeed responsible for their behavior, the tools to manage the chemical imbalances in their brain chemistries are difficult to obtain. Health insurance companies hate to cover mental illness and addiction because these are chronic conditions, difficult to accurately diagnose, and expensive to treat. While treatment is available for the wealthy, it is cheaper to discount the poor for their moral failures.

Much of the narrative of who among the poor are deserving and who are undeserving is framed as a judgment regarding what has come to be known as the "culture of poverty." Much is made in the media, in popular culture, in politics, and in academia of the characteristics of individuals trapped in the culture of poverty, of how those characteristics differ from those of the overclass. Much is made of explaining how the culture of poverty is intergenerational and oh so different from temporary, situational poverty, which is driven by uncontrollable circumstances. The deserving poor are those we have deemed to be in temporary poverty, who tend to look and act white and middle-class, those we are not afraid to meet alone in an elevator. And all of this makes sense, to a point.

Extensive literature, both popular and academic, attempts to define and explain the culture of poverty. This literature is written for a mostly white audience, many of whom are engaged in making and implementing public policy and providing services to the poor.

In addition, a great deal of popular literature, the subject of early morning news and talk shows, tries to explain the culture of poverty to the public at large while at the same time holding the poor culpable for their own poverty.

It is not unusual for popular analyses to rely on heavily racialized prejudices about the nature of poor people, specifically targeting poor communication styles and lack of the right degree of assertiveness in pursuing one's goals as causes of intergenerational poverty. There is enough semi-scientific evidence to seem to support these assertions.

Malcolm Gladwell, in "The Trouble with Genius, Part 2," (in *Outliers*, 2008) talks about the necessity of an attitude of entitlement to succeed in contemporary America. Relying on the work of Annette Lareau, he describes how class differences in assertiveness styles learned in childhood make it possible to negotiate bureaucracies and deal with authority figures in order to obtain favorable outcomes. He compares the stories of Chris Langan, a genius from a poor family, who is unable to hang on to a scholarship or get his class times changed to accommodate his lack of access to transportation, to the story of Robert Oppenheimer, the physicist who headed the American effort to develop the nuclear bomb and who early in his Harvard career tried to poison his tutor.

Langan, who had tremendous potential as a mathematician, ended up dropping out of college. Oppenheimer, after lengthy negotiations at Harvard, was put on probation and required to see a psychiatrist. The major difference, according to Malcolm, is that Langan, raised in a poor family, communicated poorly, acted submissively in the face of authority, and was too quick to resign himself to failure. Oppenheimer, who was raised in one of the wealthiest neighborhoods in Manhattan, learned early on how to be engaging and to negotiate for what he wanted out of circumstance and life.

Where these analyses, both popular and academic, fail is in denying the existence of real political, cultural, and economic conditions that remain out of one's individual control and constrain one's choices. The reality is that for people in certain circumstances, deferential behavior is a survival skill. And while the case can be made for the individual who rises above circumstances by learning to be more assertive, it cannot be the answer for an increasingly stratified society.

When I got a job in a bank, shortly after putting myself through college, my supervisor asked me to do something, I don't remember what. What I do remember is her quipping "Well, it never hurts to ask." This idea stopped me dead in my tracks, and I wanted more than anything to find a way to live a life where that statement was true. Because in my lived experience, it was never true. Questioning my alcoholic meant violence. Questioning my case worker meant a type of scrutiny that could mean loss of benefits and starvation and homelessness. It took me a long time to realize that people who gave me well-meaning advice really weren't suggesting I take actions that threatened my survival. They simply had no clue.

In the absence of acknowledgment of legitimate causes for behavioral choices, the argument that choices are individual and the result of deficient moral fiber reads as reasonable. In addition, this literature provides an objectifying distance, where those who want to "help" the poor are in no danger of being mistaken for a member of poverty culture, no matter what their own economic circumstances.

There is even a rather large cottage industry that explains to the overclass what the underclass is all about. One of the worst offenders is Ruby Payne's self-published *A Framework for Understanding Poverty*, which is reported to have sold over eight hundred thousand copies. Her book and onsite workshops are in great demand at public schools, which are struggling to effectively teach poor children and at the same time comply with the rules of the "No Child Left Behind Act," which includes specific measures for economically poor children. The "No Child Left Behind Act" created a category of students termed economically disadvantaged, whose test scores are uniquely monitored by the US Department of Education. This requires the schools to come up with effective ways to define and separately monitor economically poor students. Payne makes assertions about what she terms the "hidden rules" of people who live in poverty. These are designed to give middle-class teachers a framework for understanding their poor students. One of the most widely distributed portions of her work is a checklist (and oh, do teachers love a checklist!) that purports to tell us what skills we need to be able to live as poor, middle class, or wealthy. Skills needed to live in poverty are largely associated with at the very least immoral and at worst criminal behaviors. The case studies used to illustrate her points are predominantly stories of people of color, even though most of the people in poverty are white. Her checklist also contains items that evoke common stereotypes about class and color.

You know you can survive in poverty if:

- You know how to get someone out of jail.
- You know how to move in half a day.
- You know how to get a gun, even if you have a police record.

You know you can survive in the middle class if:

- You know how to help your children with their homework and do not hesitate to call the school if you need additional information.
- You know how to decorate the house for the different holidays.
- You know how to order in a nice restaurant.

You know you can survive in wealth if:

- You can read a menu in French, English, and another language.
- You are on the boards of at least two charities.
- You know the hidden rules of the Junior League.

A lucrative tautology is created where the narrative of the culture of poverty informs policy, which creates a market for information and training, which feeds into the original narrative and the unconscious prejudices of the public. Racializing these so-called "hidden truths" enforces implicit racism and makes it even more acceptable to refuse to talk about the economic and political conditions that create poverty, in favor of talking about moral deficits.

Activism

By the time I left my violent, alcoholic husband I had internalized a view of myself that is recognizable to me in Payne's "hidden truths." I don't trust people in authority. I don't trust people. I don't even trust myself. But, don't make the mistake of interpreting my armor as indifference.

I've spent enough time with people who are untrustworthy to doubt my own ability to reasonably judge people. The most untrustworthy of all were those people in authority who were supposed to "help" me and inevitably blamed me. I don't blame them, understand, because they were swimming in the narrative they had been taught. They couldn't understand my behavior because they were sure they would never have made my choices. Unfortunately, the choices we make can only be made from the choice sets in front of us. If the entire choice set is bad, we make bad choices.

I can't go forward here without talking about the relation between poverty and violence. And again, it is not what you think. Poor people are not more prone to violence than the overclasses, although they do have fewer resources available to deal with violence. Poverty itself is a kind of violence.

I remember an Al-Anon discussion from years ago. We struggled to decide what kind of violence and how much was bad enough that you could choose to leave. If someone hit you in an alcoholic blackout did it count? If someone threatened your life on a daily basis but never actually hit you did it count?

I know the answers to these questions might seem glaringly obvious to you. But we were raised believing that marriage was a commitment not to be walked away from, that home is the place where they always have to take you back. What you may not be able to see is that leaving wasn't just about physical safety. It was about finding a way to be the persons we were meant to be, about finding a way to do what was right no matter the obstacles. It wasn't about physical safety, it was about our ability to live up to the morality we believed in and the commitments we made.

I will say this about leaving my violent alcoholic and ending up on welfare when he refused to pay child support: being on welfare was worse. The many small daily humiliations of asking for enough assistance so your children could eat a couple of times a day, most days of the week, was worse.

This is the great violence of the myth of the undeserving poor. It isn't that you believe it. It's that you convince us to believe it. I don't think you do it because you are cruel. I think you do it because you believe the narrative and you think that if you keep us at an objectifying distance you will be safe.

But I am afraid we are closer to each other than you may choose to believe. The border to poverty is much easier to cross than the border to wealth. And it really is simply about the money. People are poor because they haven't got any money, not because they don't have the moral fiber to make the right choices. Denying us cannot make you safe.

Many solutions have been proposed that would in fact have a positive effect on reducing the rates of poverty, including increasing the earned-income tax credit and implementing universal healthcare. I believe the activist work to make these happen is important, but I also believe that efforts to change this damning narrative, to tell the stories of the people we would prefer remained invisible, to connect with people across class borders (not like-minded people, just people) is also supremely activist and necessary work.

There was a point in my life when my literal survival depended on the people who had been through what I had been through, people who knew why it is impossible to believe in yourself. We believed in each other instead.

This is the thing that keeps bringing me back to WisCon. I believe in the power of the written word, and I believe in the power of story. I believe WisCon and the people who come here have a role to play. We choose whose stories to believe. We have the power to make new stories. We have the power to change the narrative.

Notes

On the use of the term "Eskimo": The Inuit people of Canada's Northwest Territories, Nunavut, Nunavik, and Nunatsiavut have rejected the use of the term Eskimo and prefer to be called Inuit. The Alaskan Inuit, Inupiaq, and Yupik continue to refer to themselves as Eskimo or Alaskan Natives. Mr. Senungetuk, who is himself Inupiaq, uses the term Eskimo when he tells the above story. Eskimo was in all certainty the term used in the textbook to which he refers.

Sources

Bomer, Randy, Joel E. Dworin, Laura May, and Peggy Semingson"Miseducating Teachers about the Poor: A Critical Analysis of Ruby Payne's Claims about Poverty," 2008, Teachers College Record, The Voice of Scholarship in Education, http://www.tcrecord.org/content.asp?contentid=14591

Gladwell, Malcolm. *Outliers, The Story of Success*. New York: Little Brown, 2008.

Harrington, Michael. *The Other America.* New York: MacMillan, 1962.

Mishel, Lawrence. The Wedges Between Productivity and Median Compensation Growth, *Economic Policy Institute, Issue Brief #330*, April 26, 2012, http://www.ritholtz.com/blog/2012/05/the-wedges-between-productivity-and-median-compensation-growth/.

Murray, Charles. *Losing Ground: American Social Policy, 1950-1980.* New York: Basic Books, 1984.

Senungetuk, Joseph E. *Give or Take a Century: An Eskimo Chronicle.* San Francisco: The Indian Historian Press, 1971.

The "could you survive checklist" can be accessed at aha! Process, Inc. A Ruby Payne Company http://www.ahaprocess.com/News_Articles/NewsArticle_04292001-c.html.

Reinvent the Future, Change the World

I grew up Catholic in a paper mill town. In the 1950s. There were few things, as a girl, I could imagine growing up to be: a housewife or a nun. I didn't really want to grow up to be either. Then I discovered Sue Storm and Meg Murry.

They say the golden age of Science Fiction was when you were ten. When I was ten Stan Lee wrote the first issue of Fantastic Four.[1] Marvel Comics introduced something new to the comic world—characters who were no longer merely iconic. They were real messy human beings. They struggled between good and evil. They made mistakes and tried to recover from them. They were complex, or at least the boy characters were.

For the first year of the Fantastic Four, Sue Storm's only power was the ability to make herself invisible. Her other powers of the mind were added later, some of them much later. This didn't seem odd to ten-year-old, paper mill-town me. I loved her. I practiced invisibility. I dreamed that if no one caught me doing the brave or unusual, I might, might, might be able to get away with something wonderful in my life. I've never forgiven Stan Lee.

1 Stan Lee and Jack Kirby, *The Fantastic Four*, Marvel Comics 1961-1962.

It was Mrs. Black the librarian who made me read *A Wrinkle in Time*.[2] Apparently, she thought I needed role models. One little lady, in my whole little town, trying to fight stereotypes on her own, one child at a time.

One of the ways to suppress women's writing, according to Joanna Russ, is to declare "She wrote it, but she's an anomaly."[3] This also applies to characters in books. Meg Murry was an anomaly. Her mother was an anomaly. Meg Murry's mother was an actual, working, scientist. I was used to working mothers of course, though they were never called that. My Aunt Gerry always worked, but she never had a job. She was a housewife, and she worked for "pin money."

I loved Meg because I didn't know anyone like her. I couldn't believe she was real. This is a tactic not only used to suppress women's writing, but also to delegitimize all accomplishments of marginalized groups. Any individual accomplishment is an outlier and cannot change the so-called facts of popular stereotypes. Even when I saw myself represented, I couldn't see *me*. I saw an anomaly that by definition couldn't be me.

For those of us who live in the margins, who live in liminal space for reasons of color, race, gender, poverty, disability, family violence, we learn early on to weave our way in and out of reality. Melissa Harris-Perry talks

2 Madeleine L'Engle, *A Wrinkle in Time*, Farrar, Strauss & Giroux, 1963.

3 Joanna Russ, *How to Suppress Women's Writing*, University of Texas Press, 1983:

"She didn't write it. She wrote it, but she shouldn't have. She wrote it, but look what she wrote about. She wrote it, but she wrote only one of it. She wrote it, but she isn't really an artist and it isn't really art. She wrote it, but she had help. She wrote it, but she's an anomaly. She wrote it, but…"

about living in the crooked room,[4] about the difficulty of reconciling one's experience of reality with the version society imposes. As social creatures we need the shared reality of what it is to be a human being. But, we also need recognition for who we are as unique individuals. When we cannot reconcile who we are with the stereotypes imposed upon us, it can have severe consequences on our ability to function productively in society. But, there is even more to it than this.

For me, the story of science fiction is the story of learning to live in the crooked room. I was drawn to stories of the outsider, of the loner, of the outcast. There were so many stories about that loner, though. The loner, invariably a white dude, fought The Powers That Be and won. The loner lived squarely outside of the crooked

4 Melissa Harris-Perry, *Sister Citizen*, Yale University Press, 2011, p. 29:

"When they confront race and gender stereotypes, black women are standing in a crooked room, and they have to figure out which way is up. Bombarded with warped images of their humanity, some black women tilt and bend themselves to fit the distortion. It may be surprising that some gyrate half-naked in degrading hip-hop videos that reinforce the image of black women's lewdness. It may be shocking that some black women actors seem willing to embody the historically degrading image of Mammy by accepting movie roles where they are cast as the nurturing caretakers of white women and children. It may seem inexplicable that a respected black woman educator would stamp her foot, jab her finger in a black man's face, and scream while trying to make a point on television, thereby reconfirming the notion that black women are irrationally angry. To understand why black women's public actions and political strategies sometimes seem tilted in ways that accommodate the degrading stereotypes about them, it is important to appreciate the structural constraints that influence their behavior. It can be hard to stand up straight in a crooked room."

room. Because he was male, because he was white, we were already primed to know that he would win. Science fiction never filled me with that "sensa wunda." There were lots of loners in imaginary space, but I read to learn how the outcast survived.

Perry was talking specifically about the internal inconsistency of being a black woman in America, about the intersection of black and female, the discrimination assigned to both categories, but also the interstitial discriminations that apply only to black women. Intersectionality is always more than the sum of its parts.

But, I recognize that particular disjunct anyway. I am drawn to the stories of other marginalized people. I too, quest for recognition. Diana Pho said about her reading of science fiction, "… here's another truth valid in my life: when I didn't see myself in a mirror, I smashed it and saw myself in the pieces."[5]

I'm trying to keep my footing here. I take what I can get.

As my teens ended I veered even further from the classless, raceless, genderless protagonist. You see, I got pregnant at nineteen, at the height of the sexual revolution. We thought we knew better. We fought for birth control and abortion rights. We read *Our Bodies Ourselves.*[6] We talked about female orgasm. We thought we could find the one true fix. When women of color asked for a more inclusive definition of reproductive rights, white women demanded that we solve the problem of *when* we become pregnant, and all the rest would fall into place. We believed a narrative about choice, choice simplified.

5 Diana Pho, "Breaking Mirrors," http://www.jimchines.com/2015/03/breaking-mirrors-pho/.

6 Boston Women's Health Book Collective, *Our Bodies, Ourselves: A Book by and for Women*, Touchstone, 1976.

Ahh, white women and the sexual revolution. We thought we could control and celebrate and experience our own sexuality, overcoming the virtuous woman stereotype. We rebelled against her as a universal, not knowing (unwilling to recognize) that women of color, particularly black women, were never recognized as virtuous. We said we wanted sexuality without consequences, we only understood consequences imposed by misogyny. We refused to talk about sexualized racism against black women. There wasn't even a word for that until 2010 when Moya Bailey coined the word misogynoir.[7]

Then, I became a mom. The white feminist narrative betrayed me, or I betrayed it, depends on who you talk to. I guess. I crossed a border.

I've been a mom as long as I've been a grownup, longer probably. You don't see a lot of moms in science fiction. The first mom *I* ever saw was Jerry in Barry B. Longyear's "Enemy Mine."[8] (He died in childbirth, by the way. I lived.)

"We become particularly—and viciously—hungry for narrative when we are those who live in the unstable margins of the world," Claire Light writes. "It is not that you cannot have a story without conflict, but rather that without conflict, you don't *need* a story."[9]

---

7 Mysogynoir is a termed coined by Moya Bailey to refer to the way anti-blackness and misogyny combine to malign Black women. http://moyazb.tumblr.com/post/84048113369/more-on-the-origin-of-misogynoir.

8 Barry B. Longyear, "Enemy Mine," *Manifest Destiny*, Berkley Books, NY, 1980.

9 Claire Light, "Girl in Landscape, How to Fall into a Politically Useless Narrative Rut and Notions of How to Get Back Out," *Narrative Power, Encounters, Celebrations, Struggles*, ed. L. Timmel Duchamp, Aqueduct Press, 2010, p. 227.

"Enemy Mine" was told from the point of view of Willis Davidge, that loner we were talking about. This one didn't win, though. Through his relationship with Jeriba Shigan and Jerry's child, Davidge crossed the border from loner to outcast. I loved that story, too. I still cry when I re-read it.

But, here are a few things that stick out for me now. Jerry is an outsider through his role as the alien being in a war between humans and aliens. His alien status is pressed home when Davidge has a flashback to military training and the Drac are referred to with transphobic and ablest slurs. The use of these slurs does an odd double duty that we often see in fiction. By using these slurs, which even in the eighties "educated" people read as "bad," we know that the Powers That Be on the human side were also "bad." Not a stretch. This is a common sf trope, that the loner must fight the evil Powers That Be.

But, the alien being is also successfully othered, relegated to permanent outsider status through these very same slurs, because we have already agreed in the common wisdom of civilized, hierarchical societies that being trans is "icky" and that most of us would choose death over being a "retard." The literary technique only works if at some level we either believe or have internalized these notions. We do not challenge the stereotypes as applied to the Drac as much as we challenge the stereotypes when applied to Davidge. We accept that Davidge is being treated unjustly because he is associated with marginalized groups of which he is not a member. The marginalization of the Drac is only seen as wrong when seen through the white gaze[10] of Davidge's experience.

10 The white gaze is the act of centering observation in whiteness. Whiteness is considered the normal state or the unmarked state. Whiteness does not need to be remarked on,

Internalization of these notions, these notions of who is othered and who is the loner destined to win against all odds, prompts the reader to accept stereotypes. Stereotypes, even when presented as negative, are reinforced in the reading of the tale. We believe we are rejecting damaging stereotypes (good on us) at the same time that we embrace them to give meaning to the overall arc of the story.

Jerry's othering was further emphasized when the African-American actor Louis Gossett Jr. was cast in the movie to play Jerry, following a common movie/TV trope of talking about racism by metaphor in a world where all the humans are white.

Why are African-Americans always cast to play the alien? Oh you say, not always. Yeah, yeah I hear it— Will Smith.[11] To paraphrase Joanna Russ, "they did it, but there can only be one of them." African American casting in science fiction exists to make a *point*. White movie goers are able to talk about racism without talking about racism, proving that "we are not Racist."™

But, there is another pernicious danger to the lack of representation: not only how we recognize ourselves but also how we see others. Science fictional and fantastic tropes are common these days in popular culture. The days of the lonely geek reading *F&SF* and *Analog* and *Azimov's* and comic books, and getting A's in science class and math and Latin, and being outcast by the cheerleading clique are long gone.

How can people define themselves without a narrative that matches their experience? How do we see marginalized people who have only been defined for us

---

but every other race is remarkable only in its relationship to whiteness.

11 Oops. That's a little dated. I mean John Boyega.

by unrelenting, popular narratives? How do we learn to interact with people othered in popular culture if not through popular narrative? When marginalized Americans appear at all in our fiction and movies, they are presented in stereotypical ways, and the narrative reinforces the notion that it is the individual behaviors of the marginalized that are responsible for the existence of the stereotype. But make no mistake: representation is about more than hurt feelings. Representation matters because ultimately lives depend on it.

White people live in a white bubble. I'm gonna tell you a funny story about the white bubble. Except it's not funny, and it's not just a story.

Let's start with mothers. I don't remember when being a mother didn't frighten me. I knew I was too young, maybe. My babies were too perfect. When I brought my oldest child home from the hospital, I cried. She was so perfect. She was just so absolutely perfect. Anything I did to or for her could only inevitably change her for the worse.

When something tragic happens to somebody's child, it touches every parent's fears for their own children. People talk about "a parent's worst nightmare." We empathize with those suffering through this nightmare. This nightmare terrorizes the community of parents. I didn't know this when my children were small, but black mothers have different nightmares than white mothers.

I had three kids, a marriage that failed, a life to put together, somehow. My children's upbringing was, shall we say, not what I wished for them. They were wild teenagers. They broke curfew, took risks. They were acting out against leftover anger. I spent their teenage years in constant fear of what would happen to them when I didn't know where they were, what trouble they were getting into.

Spoilers. They survived. They grew into adults with their own families, their own fears, their own challenges. They made it through their teenage years. Where there's life there's hope.

My elder son acted out in the same ways his older sister had. He'd call me in the middle of the night from halfway across Madison looking for a ride home. I told myself, "At least he's a boy. At least I don't have to worry about some stranger hurting him when I don't know where he is." I told this to another mother, a black mother. "Well, you can say that," she said. "It's not true for us."

A prick in the bubble.

My grandson is the same age Trayvon Martin would be if he had not been murdered on February 26, 2012. At that time Rie was in high school, doing high school things, chasing girls, arguing with his parents, playing basketball, getting A's in courses that engaged him and barely turning up for others. He was stopped by the police regularly on his way home from school or the library. He was one of only two black kids in his class and the only Asian kid. In a town with a population of a little over two thousand, police requests to know who he was and where he was going rang hollow. They knew who he was. He was suspicious because he existed, black in a white town.

I doubt Trayvon's death would have hit me so hard if it hadn't been for Rie. I could have gone on believing that a mother's/grandmother's worst nightmare was the unexpected, unexplainable death. I didn't know about the fear of the expected death.

Most of Rie's family is white. We are late to this party. We wish this party didn't exist. This party is no fun at all.

My daughter has become the mother Mikki Kendall described: "There's a certain horrible routine you go through after you hear that a police officer has shot a Black youth. You check on your kids first. Even if the shooting wasn't in your city, there's still a moment where you need to be sure that they are okay. Then, the waiting starts: Who was the child? Do you know his/her family? ...even if it isn't your baby, it is *someone's* baby bleeding, or worse yet, already gone."[12] Another prick in the bubble.

Most white people do not interact with people of color on a daily basis. We see more portrayals of young black men as gangsters and thugs than we see of young black men in real life. We see more portrayals of young black women as single mothers and drug addicts than we do young mothers in real life. We are convinced they do not feel their motherhood the same way we do, certainly not the same way we would if we found ourselves in unfortunately similar circumstances.

When we do interact with black people in real life, we force honorary membership in the unmarked state[13] onto them. They seem no different than white people to us (we don't see color). We insist they are anomalies. We

12 Mikki Kendall, "The Worry and the Wait for Justice: What it Feels Like to be a Black Mother Right Now," *Common Dreams*, http://www.commondreams.org/views/2014/12/03/worry-and-wait-justice-what-it-feels-be-black-mother-right-now, 2014.

13 "The unmarked state—Possessing demographic characteristics considered "unremarkable" by the dominant culture." Nisi Shawl and Cynthia Ward, *Nisi Shawl and Cynthia Ward on ROAARS and the Unmarked State*, http://www.booklifenow.com/2010/03/nisi-shawl-and-cynthia-ward-on-roaars-and-the-unmarked-state/ These characteristics typically include: white, male, cisgendered, straight, able-bodied.

deny lived experience and agency in a single thought. To paraphrase Russ again, they lived it, but they're an anomaly. Our stereotypes remain intact. Physical segregation is a part of it. But even with proximity, black parents are not seen as a part of our community, the community of the unmarked state, the human community.

Knowing people of color has never prevented white people from making racist assumptions when confronted with the repeating tragedy of another black person shot by a white cop: he shouldn't have been there; he shouldn't have been doing whatever it was he was doing; if he wasn't doing anything bad at the time, he must have done something bad in the past; he shouldn't have been dressed the way he was—that led the police to the reasonable assumption of a or b above; he shouldn't have lived where he lived—that neighborhood is a known hostile environment.[14]

On August 9, 2014, Michael Brown was shot by a white cop in Ferguson, Missouri. His body was left in the street for hours. His mother was prevented from going to him.

White people imagine that if Michael had simply stepped onto the sidewalk when asked, everything would have been different. He would be alive today. We conveniently forget that cops don't patrol white neighborhoods policing jaywalkers. But if they did, we tell ourselves, we

14 Officer Darren Wilson called the area where he shot Michael Brown a "hostile environment…There's a lot of gangs that reside or associate with that area. There's a lot of violence in that area, there's a lot of gun activity, drug activity, it is just not a very well-liked community. That community doesn't like the police." Rachel Clark and Mariano Castillo, "Michael Brown Shooting: What Darren Wilson told the Ferguson Grand Jury," CNN, http://www.cnn.com/2014/11/25/justice/ferguson-grand-jury-documents/index.html, Nov. 2014.

would behave responsibly, the police would be reasonable, everything would be OK. We want to believe that the world is essentially fair. We keep this particular myth of fairness intact by divorcing individual actions from circumstances and by making judgments based on the consequences of being white in the white community.

So the news came out that Michael was stopped for jaywalking. He was insolent and disrespectful. Soon video footage surfaced of somebody who may or may have been him shoplifting a handful of five-dollar items from a convenience store. He shoved a man who tried to stop him leaving the store. This is evidence of his "thug" nature. Claire Light again: "There is no 'there' there until you build the narrative. Story doesn't reflect reality, it *creates* it."[15]

We say wait for all the facts before rushing to judgment, even though the only way to square that particular circle is to leave out most of the facts, to rearrange their order into a predetermined narrative. Once we know the timeline, we can ignore that according to Darren Wilson's initial report, he was unaware of the incident later reframed as a "strong-armed robbery"[16] at the time of the jaywalking stop.

---

15 Claire Light, Ibid.

16 "In an afternoon press conference, Ferguson, Mo. Police Chief Thomas Jackson said Wilson did not initially make a connection between the robbery and Brown, whose death spurred violent protests and unrest in the St. Louis suburb over the past week. 'Wilson stopped Brown and a friend because they were in the middle of the street, blocking traffic,' Jackson said. Yamiche Alcindor, Marisol Bello, and Aamer Madhani, "Chief: Officer noticed Brown carrying suspected stolen cigars," USA Today, August 15, 2014: http://www.usatoday.com/story/news/usanow/2014/08/15/ferguson-missouri-police-michael-

There is a loop playing in Lesley McSpadden's, Michael Brown's mother's head. I see it in her face. I am haunted by it. Where would we be if white mothers were able to put themselves in McSpadden's place? What would be different if we considered McSpadden a member of the community of mothers, if we empathized with her grief, if we shook our heads at the worst nightmare a mother can imagine? What if that look on her face resonated with all mothers?

She has the look my sister had when my nephew Nick died. Nick went to the emergency room with nausea and vomiting. He never came home. It is hard to process something that you so desperately want not to be true, something in your life that is so fundamentally wrong. My brother-in-law just shook his head. The only phrase he could utter was "Terrible. Just Terrible." Most of the sympathetic, hopefully comforting things people had to say just made him angry.

In the days that followed, we sat around my sister's dining-room table, talking about Nick, remembering Nick. Remembering Nick as a child, a teen, a young adult, the potential that was lost, the wedding my sister would never be able to go to. Good and bad, we had a shared sense of the whole of him, the him we were determined not to lose. My sister and I became unusually close. Even though we lived in the same town, we had seen very little of each other in the preceding twenty years. She said to me, "This is Nick's gift to us. That we've become close again."

It is difficult to process the unexpected death. I can't imagine the grief involved in processing the expected death, the death that seems inevitable. The death that is

---

brown-shooting/14098369/. Note how the title of the article adopts the new narrative.

the black mother's worst nightmare. Except I can. Another prick in the bubble.

McSpadden's son was stolen from her twice. In interviews she struggled to fight the narrative that has been woven to justify her child's death at the hands of a white cop. White America denied the good and bad of him, the lost potential, the hopes and fears of his parents. He was not a whole person, a whole son. He was rebranded thug.

This is *the* common narrative surrounding the deaths of black people in similar circumstances. Here is the story arc: The unimaginable happens. A tragic circumstance. We struggle to understand why. New facts come in. The victim is actually the villain. Order is restored. Confidence in the power of the state is restored.

Michael's mother is required to grieve in public spaces, is required to justify the existence of her son, rather than honoring him, remembering the best of him. She defends him in public by saying this is not the Michael we knew, yes he had his problems, but he was a good kid. If white people were truly colorblind, any parent of a teenager would be familiar with his problems, including the shoplifting, including the hip-hop music. (OMG Motley Crue roaring out of my daughters' bedroom in the nineties.)

Another prick in the bubble.

And then there's Tony Robinson, unarmed Tony Robinson, killed by a white police officer three doors down from my daughter's house in a transitional (gentrifying) Madison neighborhood on March 6, 2015. I didn't know Tony Robinson. But, by now I do know Tony Robinson.

If misdemeanors deserved the death penalty, if due process was irrelevant where wild teens were concerned, if young adults were routinely shot for being high and behaving erratically on a Friday night in college towns, white mothers would be terrified.

The familiar story surrounds Tony's death. The police officer who was called—to help him, by the way—was afraid for his life after confronting him. We do know that Tony was having a bad reaction to hallucinogenic mushrooms, that he was running in and out of traffic, that he punched someone in the head, and that his friends made the first 911 call. At the time Officer Matt Kenny first confronted Tony he had been told that Tony was probably unarmed and likely intoxicated.

Kenny chased Tony into the stairwell of his home (where dashcam footage couldn't follow). Everything that happened next happened in less than half a minute. According to the available dashcam footage,[17] Kenny entered the apartment alone, and within roughly eighteen seconds shots were fired, and Kenny backed out of the stairwell, back into view of the dashcam, firing a final shot. Tony can be seen sliding out feet first. Additional police officers arrived on the scene almost immediately.

In his statement Kenny says he opened fire after being punched while at the top of the stairs. He does not know how he got back to the bottom of the stairs. I find myself wondering, how in the world did he get to the top of the stairs in under ten seconds?

There are unsubstantiated reports that Kenny was told to wait for the backup that was moments away before entering the apartment; however, in his grand jury testimony Kenny explains that he heard noises that indicated someone might be in danger, that "he heard a dis-

---

17 "Tony Robinson Shooting: Wisconsin Officials Release Dashcam Footage," *The Guardian*, May 13, 2015, http://www.theguardian.com/us-news/2015/may/13/tony-robinson-shooting-wisconsin-dashcam-footage-released.

turbance coming from the upstairs apartment, including noises that sounded 'like a fist hitting something' and a person yelling, 'What are you going to do now, bitch?,'"[18] and that that is what prompted him to enter without waiting. He can be heard on the dashcam footage shouting "there is somebody up there" as additional officers arrive on the scene.

Without being mind-readers we will never know if Kenny really thought there were multiple people in the apartment and if he really thought he was entering the apartment to prevent imminent violence, or if it was something else that made him repeat the common narrative justifying officer-involved shootings.

He contends that he became "afraid for his life" before he started shooting, but how long before, really? If we simply take his statements at face value, it is apparent that adrenaline and fear had more to do with his interpretation of events than the chain of events did. There was no one else in the upstairs apartment.[19]

In two US Supreme Court cases, Tennessee v. Garner, 1985, and Graham v. Connor, 1989, the standards governing police use of escalation of force were revised by the Supreme Court to a more subjective measure. The current standard is the level of danger the officer surmises at the time of an encounter and the split-second assumptions he makes about the suspect.[20] In a society

18 Nico Savidge, "No Charges Against Officer," *Wisconsin State Journal*, May 13, 2015, http://host.madison.com/wsj/news/local/crime_and_courts/madison-police-officer-matt-kenny-cleared-in-shooting-of-tony/article_428b0cf9-da97-5951-9936-2f699547ba3f.html.

19 Ibid.

20 Carol D. Leonigg, "Current law gives police wide latitude to use deadly force," Washington Post, Aug. 28, 2014, https://www.washingtonpost.com/politics/current-law-gives-police-

informed by the racist idea that black people are more prone to violence and less able to feel pain, this measure is repeatedly lethal.

In the weeks prior to Tony's death, there had been a number of non-fatal shootings in Madison. Madison Police Chief Michael C. Koval attributed these to increased

---

wide-latitude-to-use-deadly-force/2014/08/28/768090c4-2d64-11e4-994d-202962a9150c_story.html.

"The first of the Supreme Court rulings that still govern law enforcement policies nationwide on the use of deadly force is *Tennessee v. Garner.* In the 1985 case, the court concluded that police officers could not shoot at a fleeing suspect simply to prevent their escape. They could shoot, however, if they had probable cause to believe the person was a violent felon and posed a significant threat of death or serious harm to the community.

"The more overarching decision is the 1989 *Graham v. Connor* ruling, written by Chief Justice William Rehnquist and at a time when violence against police was rising amid a crack epidemic. In that case, Charlotte diabetic Dethorne Graham had rushed into a convenience store to get orange juice to stop an oncoming insulin attack but left the juice inside and left suddenly because of the long line. He asked a friend who had driven him to the store to instead drive him to another friend's house for food.

"Charlotte city police officer M.S. Connor, suspicious at Graham's hasty exit, followed him and his friend, stopped them for questioning and didn't believe Graham's story about being diabetic. As Connor was checking by radio with the store, Graham got out of his car and passed out briefly. Backup officers arrived, told Graham to shut up and rammed his head into a patrol car while throwing him in the back of it.

"Graham sustained minor injuries and argued that the officer's use of force was excessive. But the Supreme Court found that the officer's actions were justified because he reasonably believed the force he was using was necessary to prevent or detect a crime in progress."

gang activity and assured the Madison community that the police force was being placed in a heightened state of alert. "Chief Koval says the shooting at West Towne Mall has taken this violence to a whole new level with hundreds of innocent bystanders put in harms [sic] way. 'We are going to bring every investigative resource we have legally to make those folks accountable. It's no longer a time to have a "pity party." Now it's time to make those people accountable,... While I'm all about looking at root causes and how we can be helpful, there's a time when "my gang" is going to have to come down and come down hard in holding people accountable,' Koval explains."[21]

Coded language in Koval's comments about gangs in Chicago, Beloit, and Milwaukee referencing "those people" make it clear to the community that Koval is talking about black male youth. It is inconceivable that this heightened state of alert did not translate to a heightened sense of danger when answering a call regarding a young black male suspect in a transitional west side neighborhood that has as many poor people of color as it has white students.

After the shooting Chief Koval congratulated the Madison Police Department on their response to protests and their ability to keep the demonstrations peaceful, as though failure of the police to incite the community to riot was a singular and praiseworthy achievement. Predictably, the white community called for the black community to wait until all the facts were in before rushing to judgment.

---

21 Gordon Severson, "Madison police say recent shootings are gang related and likely connected," WKOW.com, March 1st and March 16th, 2015, http://www.wkow.com/story/28233444/2015/03/01/madison-police-say-recent-shootings-are-gang-related-and-likely-connected.

On the night Tony was killed, his aunt Lorien Carter spoke to the neighborhood crowd gathered in front of the apartment building where he was shot. She said: "Here in our little bubble of Madison, WI… I want y'all to know, that for minorities, we are [in one of] the top five worst places to live. But we are [also in one of the] three happiest cities to be in. So who is it happy for?" "They're going to frame this so that it's the black kid's fault," said Craig Spaulding, father of Jack Spaulding, one of Robinson's closest friends.[22]

One of the damning pieces of evidence that came to light to justify loss of due process and summary execution for the crime of disorderly conduct while black was the fact that Tony had a previous felony conviction for armed robbery. He'd pled guilty in a plea deal and served probation.

But the felony conviction would follow him. He believed at the time he took the mushrooms that he no longer had a future. A matter of days before he died, he told his mom, "I fucked up." He said it over and over, "I fucked up, mom…I've ruined my life."

The adults in his life tried desperately to convince him that he still had a future, that he would get through this, that they would be there for him. There was a moment in time when there was hope, when there was a way out, even if he couldn't see it. I find myself unable to sleep at night feeling his despair. As long as there is life, there is hope. "I fucked up, mom," he says, "I've ruined my life." The needle is stuck there. Forever. Where is hope now?

---

22 Zoe Sullivan, "Madison police shooting offers stark reminder that city's race issues run deep," The Guardian, Mar. 8th, 2015, http://www.theguardian.com/world/2015/mar/08/madison-police-shooting-tony-robinson-race.

The white community sees the incidence of a white cop killing a black youth as anomalous, an isolated incident. Even when the white community feels the shooting is unjustified, it is a case of "one bad apple." Systemic patterns of abuse are never at fault. The scholar M. J. Hardman talks about anomalousness as it is embedded in the English language itself: "Anomalousness provides a way to dismiss, of making non-existent. By classifying as anomalous, one creates a way of not counting... These patterns continue to work until one recognizes them, names them, and decides not to use them."[23] The patterns are clearly evident, yet for white people to recognize and admit these patterns results in an immediately devastating effect on our world view. Basic notions of fairness are brought into question.

Human recognition, as described by Melissa Harris-Perry, also suffers a blow. The self-defensive response is to look for the anomalous characteristics, the characteristics that "prove" the pattern doesn't exist. And the patterns we turn to, to support our prevailing world view are the patterns we've learned from the stories we tell ourselves.

In science fiction these are the stories where white men can rise to be heroes and young black men can only be thugs. Yet, we could have a different response to the pattern of the repeated tragedies of the deaths of black people at the hands of white police officers. We could have a coming together, an empathy in the face of tragedy, a building of community. We could feel anguish in the case of the worst thing that can happen to a mother.

---

23 Anita Taylor, M. J. Hardman, & Catherine Wright, *Making the Invisible Visible, Gender in Language*, iUniverse LLC, Bloomington, 2009.

Hardman further describes anomalousness as a way to "keep us from perceiving people with whom we could form community." The question of who makes up a community and how a community is created is the central question of Octavia Butler's Parable duology.[24] Though the first novel, *Parable of the Sower*, is framed as a religious quest, creating community is its central task. When the communities formed by family and neighborhood fall apart, Lauren Oya Olamina is tasked with finding out if there is even any meaning in the concept of community for this dystopic future.

Butler seems particularly prescient in these books. As a domestic violence survivor, some violent dystopias just make more sense, to me anyway, than the shared perception white people have created. I'm not reading these books for disaster-movie heroism, mind you. I'm looking for tips on how to survive the unthinkable. Reading Butler is like reading ahead in the gaming cheat book to know if I am on the right track. If I keep using this strategy, will I beat the boss? I read dystopian fiction to find out if people like me will live till the end. Mostly we don't. But sometimes we do. Where there's life, there's hope.

There is a parallelism within the work as well as a parallel to real-world society. Olamina first turns her back on the religion her pastor father has given her. She does this because any kind of an ordered society has already turned its back on her. Although *Parable of the Sower* is written as a quasi-religious tract, finding community is the key to the new religion, and finding a society that actually works for its members is its goal. Olamina is forced to flee the gated community in which she lives after the murder of her father and after the walls are

24 Octavia Butler, *Parable of the Sower*, Book One of the Parable Series, Open Road Integrated Media, Jan. 1, 2000.

no longer sufficient to keep out the most marginalized members of what can barely be called society.

At first she looks for the specific family and friends she has lost. Eventually she makes common cause with two people whom she herself terms an unlikely pair. This is the beginning of the new community, united to follow Olamina and her new religion. The new community of the novel is created through circumstance and choice. Choosing whom to trust is key. What makes this especially difficult for Olamina is that she has inherited a birth defect of hyper-empathy. Her perception of other people's pain and despair literally cripple her.

Trust is a sensitive topic for me. When I left my abuser, I had to accept the fact that trust had failed me, that I was totally incapable of getting a read on people, so to speak. I know now that abusers do not wear their intent like a badge. People who insist that there are signs are unlikely to be survivors.

So, I don't trust anybody anymore, least of all myself. But this is not necessarily a bad thing. I never take it personally if someone chooses not to trust me. After all, it is likely what I would do if I were in their shoes. A recurring theme of black activists is the refusal of whites to accept the validity of their lived experience. Yet if white people were to trust the framing of people of color, we would have to make an enormous leap into belief in a society that is fundamentally unfair and dangerous to its citizens. But how are we to cope with something we can't even see? Wouldn't we all be stronger for recognizing the truth?

There is a loop playing in Michael Brown's mother's head: this can't be true—it must be true. I see it in her face. I am haunted by it. Like Olamina I can't *not* feel her pain. Her pain is dangerous. But, just as being a domestic violence survivor gives me the ability to know that trust is a gift and not an entitlement, as a white person I can bear witness.

So, I get why representation matters, really. It's nice to find people who look like you, who face your struggles, who triumph outside of a narrow path. It is important for young people to have role models, in fiction as well as in life. Books where people who look like me, who've been through what I've been through, mean a great deal to me. But I also seek out the books by people who do not look like me, who've survived different struggles, who aren't afraid to lift the veil of white entitlement and imagine a different future. I read to see myself. I read to see a world where my family survives. I read for a future I've been unable to imagine on my own. I read for hope.

Game Theory
(Fiction)

We couldn't stop looking back. We took our children and our children's children beyond the stars, but we could never stop looking back.

Game: Zero-sum game with a fixed payoff.

Resources on the ship are limited. This game illustrates the dominant strategy if the goal is to maximize the individual's share of resources. Ship resources (i.e., water, food, quality of berth, exercise-time allotment, entertainment equipment) are assigned a point value. Points earned in the game can be used to purchase ship resources. There are a finite number of points. For the purpose of this exercise the colonists are separated into red teams and blue teams. The games are played one-on-one, without any knowledge of the opponent's team membership or individual strategy.

↔

Project notes: I am troubled by the assumption, built into the game, that one group will always be dominant. Would it have been better to leave behind all talk of winners and losers? Who is to say what strategies will be needed by the survivors and their descendants? No one knows what challenges they will face. Is survival necessarily zero-sum?

↔

In the artificial night, some of the passengers move aimlessly in the corridors. The light on the ship is muted. Some of the passengers huddle together and hang onto each other. They are afraid of the unfamiliar movements they make in reduced gravity. They are beginning to lose the notion of up-down, back-front, past-future. Nothing reminds them of evenings at home.

The ship hums of machinery. The only natural sound is the sound of quiet voices. Fabienne Jouy absently rubs her extended belly. "Do you think they will put me to sleep to have him?" she asks, and "I never thought his father would be left behind and I would be alone." The passengers murmur sympathies. None of them know what genetics they were selected for either.

↔

Project notes: The passengers were chosen for a mix of genetic attributes that were thought likely to both maximize the chances of surviving the journey through space and of producing offspring who would thrive on planet fall. It was thought best to hide the reason for why they were chosen from the passengers. They would be free to form bonds and associations shipboard without underlying assumptions of what their role or the role of their offspring would be.

Ten percent of the assigned berths belong to passengers whose genetic records are sealed from the scientific staff. It is widely assumed that those passengers were able to purchase their berths, based on their wealth and position on the old planet. All of the ten percent identify as male.

Game: Classic Prisoner's Dilemma, a study in cooperation.

The passengers have been sorted into red teams and blue teams for this game. They will play one on one. They will know nothing about their opponent, but they will be given the opportunity to play the same opponent multiple rounds. If both players choose cooperation they will lose minimal privileges. If one chooses cooperation and one chooses self-interest, the one who chooses cooperation will lose privilege, but the one who chooses self-interest will be rewarded. If they both choose self-interest they will both lose all privileges for an extended period of time.

↔

Project notes: The engineers have told me that they expect the red team will prove to be more aggressive than the blue team. They point out that red team members have more of the same attributes as the engineers themselves—logical, physically strong, direct, argumentative, competitive, intelligent. The engineers tell me red team passengers could be trained to be engineers or physicists. I point out that the data shows that there is no statistically significant difference between choices made by members of either team. The ship captain directs me to take another look at the studies.

↔

Laure Jamais sits in the blue passenger quarters and tells a story about a time before she left the earth. "At one time," she says, "there was plenty of water in the land I come from. It pooled in lakes and flowed in rivers. One could stop anywhere along the bank and drink clean water. Animals were not raised in pens and feedlots.

They roamed the land. They ate what they found, whatever they liked to eat.

"One time a tribe of warriors left the city and wandered to a large lake. They carried machine guns and long knives. The guns had no more bullets. The warrior's clothes were dusty and torn.

"The warriors themselves smelled of sweat and blood and sorrow. They walked right down to the bank where the bears were fishing for salmon. The bears had long claws that gleamed brighter than the men's knives. They smelled the blood on the warriors' clothes and stood up tall on their hind legs. The bear closest to the first warrior reached out one of her large paws and tore out the man's throat. The bears could suddenly smell fear and fresh blood.

"The warriors were too stunned to try to outrun the bears. They couldn't outrun them anyway. The bears killed all of the warriors and began to eat them where they fell on the bank. The bears teased their bodies apart and ate what they wanted. They went to the lake to drink and their muzzles were covered in blood. There was so much blood the lake became muddy and then red. The bears ate and drank and ate and drank and fell asleep on the bank. When they awoke none of the animals could drink the water anymore."

↔

Project notes: Marthe Ephore has come to talk to me about Fabienne Jouy's fear of the ship physicians. Marthe tells me Fabienne suffers from survivor's guilt; guilt that all of her family was left behind. Marthe tells me Fabienne has accused the ship staff of kidnapping her; that she says she was *not* chosen to be saved. Marthe does not say that Fabienne is hysterical. She does not say that Fabienne is suffering from the hormones of late stage pregnancy. Marthe explains that Fabienne's family has a long sociocultural history of mistrusting authority. Marthe says that sometimes that mistrust was well-reasoned.

↔

Fabienne Jouy goes into labor on one of the blue passenger decks. No one calls the ship physicians. The passengers have tied sheets between the bulkheads and surrounded Fabienne with pillows. Some of them carry makeshift suction bags, to gather escaping fluids if artificial day turns to artificial night before Fabienne finishes giving birth.

Fabienne rolls onto her hands and knees and rocks back and forth. One of the passengers rubs her back, another feeds her chips of ice, another brushes her hair away from her face and neck. Fabienne grunts as she rocks—unh unh unh. Most of the passengers have formed a large outer circle. They breathe together in loud gusts, whoosh in, whoosh out. A breathing rhythm is established for Fabienne to follow. She is able to roll on her side and sleep between contractions.

When Fabienne rolls onto her back, the passengers at her elbows help her to a squatting position. The passengers in the outer ring breathe faster now. Whew—in; whew—out. Whew—push; whew—push. They breathe in sharp gasps and whoop loudly when Fabienne breathes out. Push push push.

↔

Project notes: The ship crew and scientific staff have met to discuss Fabienne Juoy's son. They had not expected him to be black. Someone says no one knew that Fabienne was black, she is so light skinned. Someone says maybe it was only because of the father. Someone asks Daniela Nervi, one of the ship geneticists, why the father's genetics were not tested or the fetus's. Someone says what a shame it is, we had hoped to leave problems of race and class behind us. Someone says by the time we land his descendants should look no different than anyone else's. Daniela Nervi chews her bottom lip and does not answer. I am angry. Daniela looks at me. She shakes her head. She mouths to me, not now. She mouths to me, soon.

Game:

Prisoner's Dilemma using the Nash Equilibrium it is assumed no player can benefit by changing strategy while the other players keep their strategies unchanged. Games will be played against and between teams. Passengers will be given the prior study data, which shows that red team members always play aggressively and blue team members always play cooperatively.

↔

Project notes: To obtain the best individual outcomes it is best to stay within predicted parameters, based on the team to which the passenger has been assigned. Over time players tend to perform as predicted, no matter what their initial strategy may have been. An unanticipated finding of the current game is that the passengers are not likely to trust their own experience in game strategy if it contradicts what they have been told about how the other players will perform.

↔

On the blue passenger deck Marie Serge tells the story of the goddesses Mawu, Sabulana, and Alé: "Mawu, Sabulana, and Alé have come together to decide what is to be done about the people. They have given the people the earth. They have taught the people to plant and grow food. They have taught the people to weave and to teach their children how to do all of these things to care for themselves. Mawu, Sabulana, and Alé decide it is now time to give the people the sky.

"The goddesses climb to the tops of the mountains, but they cannot reach the sky. They shed their clothes but they cannot reach the sky. Finally they shed their skin and blood and bones and fly up up up, past the moon, past the planets, past the sun."

↔

The light in the ship garden is designed for the growth of the plants. The plants cover the surface of the innermost wall of the ship. There are only plants to be seen in all directions. There are layers of plant material wound into mesh above and below. From the center of the cylinder the glow of light is seen. Here the light does not respect artificial day and artificial night. Here the light only respects the plants.

The passengers float from handhold to handhold along the winding trails of the garden. The light is pale yellow and green reflected from the mustard, radish, cabbage, broccoli, and kohlrabi. The air has a musky scent of growth mingled with decay. The recyclers are hidden behind the mesh. A passenger rubs the coarse leaves of a kohlrabi and pulls her hand away to stare at her fingertips painted green. A passenger says, "In the city I come from the public was never allowed into the gardens."

↔

In the ship garden, Daniela Nervi tells a story. "On the other side of the sun," she says, "there is a vast clear land. The goddesses have left behind everything that reminded them of the earth. They have only their spirit forms here. The goddesses approach their brother, The King of the

Gods. His throne is made of scraps of skulls and scraps of bones. They tell their brother The King of the Gods that it is time for the people to gain the sky as well as the earth. The King of the Gods laughs. He cannot see the goddesses standing before him. He cannot see their spirit forms. He hears their voices as whispers." Daniela Nervi says, "This story is from A-fri-ca."

Fabienne Jouy sits in the circle with her son on her lap. She whispers to him, "You will not be the only one. Your stories will not be forgotten. What we cannot remember you will invent." Daniela Nervi nods.

↔

Movement through space is strange to the older passengers. We are used to feeling motion relative to the impact of a stronger gravity on fluids in the inner ear. This never feels right here. This never matches what we see. We look through portholes and at viewing screens. We see candy-colored nebulas swirling on what we can't stop thinking of as the horizon. We think these nebulas and the stars should whoosh past, traveling as we are, close to the speed of light.

When we were on the earth we measured distance in hours. Most of us will not live as long as planetfall. We wonder how to adapt to this life. We cannot escape the feeling that we are constantly waiting.

↔

Project notes: The engineers and physicists are proud. The engineers and physicists say, "Without us who will fly the ship? Without us who will keep order among the passengers? Without us how will we survive on the new earth? Without us how will the new earth be seeded?" No matter how many variables are introduced to the game, it is always a dichotomy.

Game:

This game measures uncertainty by introducing additional variables. This is a trading game that identifies the maximum use value of rewards and privileges. Not every player will place the same value on each of these. This game measures the strategies individual players use to maximize their individual outcomes. The equilibrium value of the game depends upon the player's ability to recognize when the opponent assigns differing values to rewards and privileges.

↔

Project notes: I had a dream last night. I dreamt that Thesis seeded Antithesis, who gave birth to a child. Thesis said, "This child will be my reflection on the new world." Antithesis said, "This child will not be constrained by gender. This child will not be this or that. This child will find its own way." When I think about this dream, I wonder if we can ever overcome this habit of thinking first this, then that, then a new this.

↔

At one time we knew our planet could not survive. One said the problem is this. One said, no that is the problem. Another said pollution, or politics, or war. They said we will build a new world without these. One asked will women be equal on the new world? One asked, what about race? What about poverty? They told us, wait, wait, wait. Your needs are small. Your truth is not as important as the larger truth. Wait until we build the new world. Then we will listen. We can save those who see this. But first, you must wait. Never forget who has the power.

↔

Some of us wonder how long it will be before things change. Some of us wonder how far we will have to travel. Some of us thought it would be one thousand years before we found a suitable planet. We think linear games will not teach us a new way of thinking. Diametric idealism only obscures our conflicts. We think one thousand years is too long to wait.

↔

The Goddess of the Sun went to see her brother the King of the Gods. The Goddess of the Sun said, "It is time my people have the sky." The King of the Gods answered her, "The sky is mine. I will give you Death to bring to your people. When they have Death they can come worship me. When they have Death they can come and be my servants." The Goddess of the Sun took Death and left the sky. The Goddess of the Sun took Death back to the earth.

Some of the children listening ask, "What is the sun?" Some of the children listening ask, "What is the earth?" Some of the children tell us we will make up new stories. Your stories mean nothing to us.

The older passengers say, tsk tsk tsk, on the old world we would never...tsk tsk tsk, on the old world we would always.... Some of us wonder, isn't this just the same old argument?

Game:

In this game the ship crew and scientific staff have been assigned to teams and are included in the game play. The ship engineers, mathematicians, and physicists are randomly assigned to the red team. The ship economists, sociologists, and biologists are randomly assigned to the blue team. Team assignments are not based on gender.

Any gender disparity in team assignments must be the result of individual choices over which the game planners have no control.

↔

Project notes: I ask Marthe Ephore why she became a sociologist. I tell her I had wanted to be a physicist. I tell her my teachers told me I would be happier if I became an economist. They told me I was better suited to a field that was less competitive. They told me if I wanted to go to space I would need to find a way to be helpful. Marthe says she always wanted to be a sociologist. Marthe says how people interact has always seemed to her the primary problem. Marthe laughs. She tells me, I never had physics envy.

↔

Some say the ship is like a womb, carrying its children to a new world. Some say it is like a penis pushing through space to seed the new world. Some say on the old world imaginary people called aliens had round ships called U-F-Os. All of the real ships were shaped like penises. People who believed in the round ships were ridiculed. People were told those ships cannot be true because no one has really seen them. Some people said, you make them invisible by denying them. Some people said, we will be seen. No matter who flies the ship, we will fly the ship.

↔

Fabienne Jouy's great-granddaughter Sophie Jouy sits on the blue deck in a circle of students. She spreads her labia and says this is the clitoris. It is made up of a hood and a glans, connected to the crura and surrounded by erectile tissue called the bulbs of the vestibule. This is an organ solely for sexual pleasure. The penis is somewhat like this, but it is awkward, not subtle, and encases the urethra, which is unclean.

The students watching Sophie are not the same color. They are many colors or many shades of the same color. After four generations their features have not become more alike. Some of them hold hands. Some of them laugh.

↔

The young passengers no longer time their activities to coincide with artificial day. The young passengers are as comfortable in no gravity as they are in limited gravity. The young passengers have no more need for clothing in the constant temperature of the ship.

Anemone Flavien thinks it is inefficient to have to manage enough plant material to turn into fiber to clothe the whole ship. Anemone Flavien has taken to weaving plant material into pages for small books called feminaries. They are distributed to the children of the blue deck passengers, along with pens made of fibrous plant stems and filled with indigo ink. The children fill the pages with the stories they want to keep. These are stories they don't want stored on the ship computers.

↔

Project notes: The scientific staff who are members of the red team now hold separate meetings on ship policy and procedures. Only red team passengers have access to red team scientific staff. All observational study data supplied by blue team scientific staff must be vetted by red team staff. Job titles for blue team scientific staff have been downgraded. Red team passengers are working on developing a new type of game for the next session.

Game:

In this game the red team and the blue team are given different sets of rules. The red team is given access to the computers and the engineering data. The blue team is given responsibility for tending the garden, for preparing food, for childbirth, for educating children in subjects suitable to their team designation. When red team members and blue team members come of age they will be given a test. This test will determine adult team assignments. This test will be based on appropriate attributes. We are told this test is fair.

↜

Project notes: I have been told I am no longer needed for administering the game and compiling game data. I wander the garden. I wander the blue decks. I cannot unlearn what I already know.

↜

Blue deck passengers have dealt with loss and blood and death for centuries. Blue deck passengers have administered birth. They are well suited to administer death. Blue deck passengers help blue team staff break through to the red decks. Blue team staff override computer access restrictions. Blue team passengers surround them shouting, whoop, whoop, whoop. They flash weapons made of the hard and bitter stems of plants. They flash weapons made from metals scavenged from passenger decks. They are adept at suctioning the floating droplets of blood.

↜

Anemone Flavien says war will soon spread to the blue decks. Given the structure of the ship, it cannot be contained on the red decks. Anemone Flavien says we must be prepared to suffer losses.

We are prepared to run the ship. The knowledge we need is contained in the computers and the feminaries.

The knowledge of how to build a new society has yet to be invented.

Unofficial games of hand-to-hand combat are organized.

↔

Program notes: I wonder what will happen when the red team members are pushed through the airlocks. Will their bodies burst in space? Will they freeze? Will they suffocate slowly? Will they float without moving, left behind forever? I ask Daniela Nervi what she thinks will happen. I cannot watch.

↔

The recovered computer codes are used to deny access to red team members still hiding on the ship. Barricades to the garden are coded in. There is dancing, feasting, singing, yelling. There are no more teams. There is no more red. There is no more blue. We will not wear the colors of our fallen comrades. We will wear tattoos in both colors and all colors. We will no longer divide ourselves into teams.

A red team member has found his way through the electronic barricade. He is seen floating naked at the edge of the festivities. He stretches his arms straight out from his sides and turns slowly. He tells us I bear no colors now. The people pull him into a circle. They tattoo his body in all of the colors of the ship. He joins in the feasting. He sings along in the long sad keening for the fallen. Remaining members of the red team find their way to the garden. Only if they can deny the old ways of doing things are they welcomed. Only if they can commit to finding new ways are they embraced.

↔

Final program notes: Only a small handful of those with the longevity modification remain alive on the ship. I have watched one hundred generations. I wander the decks. Sometimes people ask me to tell stories of the old world. Some I remember. Some I have forgotten. Marthe Ephore and Daniela Nervi and I sip tea in the garden. I tell Marthe and Daniela I no longer feel the burden of endless waiting. I feel I am watching something new begin.

The Alien Among Us
WisCon21 Souvenir Book: Notes from the Editor

After attending my first WisCon last year, discovering for the first time the huge interactive society of fans and writers, I began to wonder where exactly I fit in this community that has touched my life for much of the past thirty-five years. Why exactly do I choose to read sf? Why in my secret heart of hearts would I like to write it someday? What exactly draws me in? What is sf?

Well, at my age, I'm not as foolish as I used to be, so I didn't try to define sf (even for myself). I did, however, try to categorize the fiction I've chosen to read. Were they considered part of the sf lexicon? If not, why not? Where to begin?

One of the panels I attended at WisCon 20 was a panel moderated by David Hartwell on "the great myths/tropes of speculative fiction." This suggested a recognizable commonality, a community represented through language. Issues were raised surrounding the role of the hero in sf, dystopic vs. triumphant fiction, does or can sf rely on other literary genres for theme? The panel discussion articulated my questions, but left them all unanswered.

What was I reading when I was twelve? My brother read sf (over my mother's objections). The classics, the stories reprinted in Hartwell's *Age of Wonder* and countless other anthologies, were the books on my little brother's shelves and so by definition uninteresting, (Could there be anything more alien to a twelve-year-old girl than a ten-year-old brother?)

I remember clearly the first sf book that I ever read. It was Madeline L' Engle's *A Wrinkle in Time.* I remember exactly why I loved that book: it wasn't the science, it wasn't the triumph (to tell you the truth I don't remember exactly how it ended); it was the fact that that little girl did whatever she darned well pleased! The world was open to her. I had such a hard time reconciling myself between the things I wanted and the thing I felt I should want.

The Age of Wonder really began for me during the late '70s, when I began reading Ursula K. Le Guin, Vonda McIntyre, Joanna Russ, Zena Henderson, and Pamela Sargent. After being involved in anti-Vietnam War activity, I realized that I was probably not going to save the world, and I turned my attentions to saving just one tortured alcoholic. This was not a wise plan.

It was the writers mentioned above who sustained me through a very dark period, who helped me believe that it was the little daily battles that were worth fighting and worth winning. My brother (the one I mentioned before) sent me Pamela Sargent's *Women of Wonder,* and on the flyleaf he wrote, "Because you are one." I believed this enough to get myself and my children out of an increasingly desperate situation.

My heroes have never been the little boys in the spaceships who conquered the alien through their bravado and mastery of the wonders of science. My heroes are the people who continue to struggle through the day-to-day.

I gathered up my children and we left their alcoholic father. The intensity of my need to keep my children safe, the events of the life we had been through together, were things not talked about in polite circles. Not at school (I had returned to college), and not at work. But, there was Nancy Kress and her wonderful story "Margin of Error." The image of the mother holding a conversation with her sister while her mind was occupied with watching the color of her daughter's lips in the wading pool (blue is bad) was precious to me. And the ending (which I will not give away) took me by surprise and made me laugh.

When my son's learning disability was diagnosed, and later my nephew's autism, there was Octavia Butler with "Speech Sounds." This was so much more than "speculation" on what could happen if something caused people to lose the ability to communicate. I knew she understood what it was like to love people who cannot understand language in the same way most people can.

WisCon 21's guests of honor are Melissa Scott and Susanna Sturgis. Scott is new to me but Sturgis is not. Melissa Scott's characters are approachable regardless of the reader's sexual orientation. They are just there, and their stories are compelling. Scott neither minimizes the discrimination her gay characters face nor makes their political struggles specific only to the gay community.

Susanna Sturgis made a life's work of bringing the gay community to sf and vice versa. It was Susanna Sturgis who gave me Joanna Russ through her late 1980s anthologies.

I remember sitting in a college literature class in the mid-eighties when the professor posed the question, "Can women write as well as men?" The boys in the class immediately tried to answer this question. Seriously? The girls, properly trained by the school systems of the Midwest, though clearly agitated did not respond. The only answer I could think of was, "Well of course women can write as well as men; it's just that men tend to write about such boring stuff." I hadn't read fiction by men for years.

This, by the way, was the professor who introduced me to Virginia Woolf, who taught me to read in Woolf's fiction her struggle between the need for respectability and the need to validate her experience through her voice. (If I'd never read Woolf, would Tiptree's "The Women Men Don't See" have held the same meaning for me?) Why isn't *Orlando* commonly classified as one of the great classics of sf? Still, he felt it was provocative to ask a question that minimized the women in the class. But, I still had the books.

I went back to Hartwell's essays and Le Guin's essays about the field. Hartwell spent a great deal of effort on classifying the trends in sf. I was still confused. As Hartwell chronicled the dissension that shook the field in the seventies, as he talked about how big the field has become and how that was probably a good thing (even if one still missed the good old days when you could read it all every year), I became less concerned with trying to fit the works that moved me into some sort of pattern. The pattern of course is personal.

I started to read men again. Some of them get it; some of them don't. Who would have thought a man would one day write a book with a theme of gender discrimination (David Brin's "Barrier Reef") and have the theme be taken matter-of-factly? Not as some over-emotional feminist tripe, but as an acceptable convention for getting a story across?

And that's the point, after all, getting the story across. And as we read the stories we discover that the alien among us is us. SF provides a place where one's gender identity, for instance, or exposure to family violence become something neither shocking, nor central to how we view each other, but a part of a very human whole. In sf's exploration of the extremes I've found a safe home, where my experiences need not be minimized for the comfort of others. Where ways of being outside of my experience become something to delight in and treasure. Where everyone's story can be believed.

Sheri Tepper Is My Hero, An Appreciation

WisCon 22: Souvenir Book: Notes from the Editor

Sheri Tepper is my hero. I say this even though I resisted reading *A Gate to Women's Country* when it first came out. It seemed like it must be another formulaic, post-apocalyptic, dystopian, sf/fantasy, with a feminist twist. This was before I was familiar enough with Tepper to realize that she likes to give her readers something more than a little twist.

The first book of hers I read was *Raising the Stones*, and this was when I realized she does something unique with the tropes of science fiction and fantasy. First of all, she ignores the guidelines. She writes pure fantasies that take place in outer space, and then her characters travel to other planets and she doesn't even *try* to solve the problem of faster than light travel. But, she does stay true to the feel of adventure and heroism, which is the hallmark of good space opera. At the same time, she does not shy away from asking (and answering) the big human questions, the questions that literature is uniquely capable of dealing with.

In *Raising the Stones* she grapples with the question of human responsibility versus free will. The thing I like best about the Hobbs Land Gods is that they *work*. They work in the way we have come to expect things to work.

When I turn on the radio and don't get any sound I say to myself, "Why doesn't this work?" When I turn on the faucet and no water comes out I say, "Now, why isn't this working?"

The Hobbs Land Gods *work* in the way one would expect God to work if you thought about it. When they are present there is no hatred, jealousy, cruelty, selfishness, or poverty. Why hasn't humanity invented gods like these before? Why have our gods always seemed vindictive or capricious? And if god is benevolent and all powerful, how can the world's many daily horrors be allowed to exist? Ah, yes, free will. Maybe it's not god after all who wants things both ways, good and bad and the power to choose between them. Maybe it's just us. Incredibly difficult questions for space opera.

This is the basic theme underscoring most of Tepper's work. In *Sideshow* she repeatedly asks the question "What is the ultimate purpose of mankind?" She doesn't shy away from the answer, either. She tells us in half a dozen words, and I find I can't help but concur with her answer.

Ah, this brings us to the other Tepper question. Am I such an avid fan because I already agree with her message? Sheri Tepper is nothing short of polemic. I haven't read any of her crime fiction, but in her sf her opinions are resoundingly clear. On the other hand, it is such a *relief* to escape, however briefly, to a world where it is safe to express such unpopular opinions as anti-abortion activists should be consigned to an endless hell of being pregnant and giving birth, or there are some things that are worse than death. And, somehow, just before these issues can become too heavy or too poignant, Tepper brings in her wonderfully self-conscious sense of humor.

But, I haven't gotten around to telling you why she is my hero, which has less to do with her body of work than with her as a person. I have to warn you, however, that most of what I know of her as a person I have made up. I read on a book jacket, somewhere, sometime, that she didn't start publishing until she had retired. (See, I'm changing the facts already. I'm sure it said "didn't start *writing* but, she must have been creating those wonderful stories all along in her mind, at least.) I have this picture of her in *my* mind sitting across her desk at Planned Parenthood talking with some very young, very scared girl. The girl is saying something like, but my parents would just kill me if they ever found out.

When Sheri is most adamant in her work about the consequences of choices, it's because she has watched certain events play themselves out time and time again. I have found myself too often in life in situations where the only choices I had were bad choices. Too many kids too young and married to an alcoholic. I'm not whining. I just want you to know that the old saying—anything that doesn't kill you, only makes you stronger—is a bunch of bunk. Unfortunately, there are events that do destroy people, events from which people never recover. I was one of the lucky ones. I had people to believe in me, to root for me when I most needed it.

I can picture Sheri sitting at that imaginary desk telling me sternly, "You have to do what's best for those kids," and then a little more gently, "Of course you're afraid, but I'll stand by you." I searched for that message daily when my children were young. Some sign that I could take care of them, raise them, make a good life for them, make a life for myself. And we did. Because, we were never entirely alone. I'm terrified by a current wisdom that blames all of society's problems on lack of individual responsibility, conveniently absolving society of any responsibility.

But, this still isn't enough to tell you why Sheri is my hero. I have always wanted to write. When I was in my twenties I was busy trying to overcome years of conditioning that said, "You made your bed, now lie in it," or "Home is the place where they always have to take you in" (applied to my alcoholic, this meant—if I didn't take care of him who would? besides he was my husband, my family). I read that Virginia Woolf said "Anybody can have babies, but only I can write my books." But, I knew that only I could care for *my* babies, and books would have to wait.

By my thirties I was raising the kids on my own, on and off welfare and back in school. Any writing I did was working toward a degree, which I hoped would land me more than a minimum-wage job. (I was an econ major. I could pretty well figure that with day care costs of $2.50 an hour for 3 kids with wages of $5.00 an hour, we weren't going to make it.) I read Joanna Russ's *How to Suppress Women's Writing* (1983) and found a long list of women writers who were unable to begin their careers until after their children were grown. I couldn't imagine putting it off that long. The need to write is daily, but sometimes it is just not paramount. I was depressed for days.

Shortly before turning forty, I discovered Sheri Tepper. She did two things for me. First, she surprised me. Maybe it was a trick, but *Gate to Women's Country* took a few turns I wasn't expecting. Oh, my expectations had been set up by Sheri's use of dystopian tropes. But, it's not just that she did something unexpected. Sheri preys on the human desire to be complacent and tells us—"not a chance, buddy." I love this. I've never had the luxury of becoming complacent. I have not mellowed as I've gotten older. Like Sheri, I hope I've become stronger and more irascible.

Second, she proved that the stories don't have to be told right away. A writer can hang onto them, and they can grow and mature as the writer grows and matures. And then when you finally have the time, when you finally can put the writing first, there the stories are. And they come tumbling out, everything you've had to say all those years. And one after the other they get better and stronger because they have that kernel of truth that cannot be invented. They haven't just come whole, made up, out of the writer's head, they come from the writer's life. And now they are a part of that dialogue between writer and reader that is informed not just by the opinions of both, but by the experiences of both. So hang on, Sheri, I've seen you do it, and I'm following right behind you.

The WisCon Coup

So, here's a thing. In the 1960s, when I was in my late teens, there was a saying "Don't trust anybody over thirty." Nowadays, apparently, people my age no longer trust anyone *under* thirty. Of course, nothing is ever as simple as that. It's easy-easy to talk about the changes in requests for diversity in Speculative Fiction as a generation gap, with ageist arguments rife on both sides. (Hah, two sides, see below.) But see, I remember when we thought we just had to wait for Nixon, Wallace, Kissinger, Hoover, Scalia (oh wait no, your generation was waiting for him) etc. to die off and then progress would win. Ooops.

This is what I call the Hegelian mistake. The idea that when you have two opposing forces (thesis/antithesis) they will always recombine to something better (synthesis) as if by magic, as if we *must* excuse historical figures (who had a vested interest in political outcomes btw) for their actions, as if we are required to forgive them as products of their time, as if all the blood sweat and tears don't matter, as if progress happens, as if waiting for change works better than fighting for it, as if popular culture is irrelevant to popular conscience.

Many of the fights in sf fandom are over what some perceive as the changing nature of fandom and of the work of sf itself. We fight over how much, when, who wins, who loses, freedom of speech written and expressed, and tone. Watch that tone, because if you use the wrong tone you deserve to lose, or so I've been told.

In the summer of 2014, WisCon was caught up in these battles in a major way. First there was the bungled Frenkel harassment incident. Coming after a string of harassment incidents that had bubbled to the surface in fandom, Frenkel's presence at WisCon 38 in a prominent, public-facing role and the failure of the ConCom to follow up on Elise Matthesen's and others' initial harassment reports caused a widening fracture. WisCon billed itself as the world's first, possibly only feminist science fiction convention. The membership felt betrayed. Many took to social media demanding answers and accountability. Debbie Notkin, who chaired the Frenkel harassment subcommittee, was accused of being complicit in protecting Frenkel because of her decades of work in the publishing industry.

A lack of systems, a lack of organizational and feminist theory, made these claims seem plausible. Debbie Notkin, Jeanne Gomoll, Jim Hudson, and others of the early/founding members of WisCon had been fighting internally for intersectional feminism within the ConCom for years. They had worked at expanding the membership of the convention and the leadership of the ConCom to include more POC and other marginalized people. Now they were being accused of taking deliberate actions that they personally abhorred.

Still, it wasn't the Frenkel incident itself that resulted in members of the ConCom resigning. It was a fracture over what to do about Richard Russell and the larger implications of that action. Richard was one of the founding members of WisCon. He was a familiar face at the registration table. Within the ConCom itself, he had been arguing against the POC safer space since it had first been proposed in 1999 for WisCon 23 and long after the ConCom had decided the issue. Why had that been allowed to go on as long as it had? It appeared that there was a core group who would always privilege their friends over the needs of POC. The structure allowing the impulse to extend that privilege to friends and only to friends came directly from attempts to follow feminist organizing principles, with insufficient feminist theory. These principles had come out of the white feminist movement of the late sixties early seventies, and their feminist counter arguments had been lost.

In January of 2015, the *Guardian* declared 2014 the year when Science Fiction and Fantasy woke up to diversity,[1] its click-bait headline insisting that fandom at large was somehow surprised. Popular media recognized diversity as something that inexorably happens, a quick win for instance after the unfortunate chainmail bikini-gate of 2013.[2] Those who fought this fight heard the implicit argument—but stop, stop, stop already. You've won. Enough. Enough change for now. For—ev—er. For those of us of a certain age we also heard— See, this happened when the time was right. Nothing *you* did ever mattered. Forget about it. We've already forgotten all about you.

And this is what hurt older white women writers, the feeling of being dismissed on both sides of the equation. Being told to wait your turn and then finally being

1 Damien Walter, "2014: The year when science fiction and fantasy woke up to diversity," *The Guardian*, Jan. 2, 2015, http://www.theguardian.com/books/booksblog/2015/jan/02/2014-year-science-fiction-fantasy-woke-up-diversity

2 Alison Flood, "Science fiction authors attack sexism amid row over *SFWA* magazine," *The Guardian*, Jun. 12, 2013, http://www.theguardian.com/books/2013/jun/12/science-fiction-sexism-sfwa

told it was too late for you. Move aside. Make way for the young.

Still, I have trouble understanding the suspicion with which this older generation, my generation of mostly white female authors and fans view the new generation. I get suspicion, mind you. I don't trust anybody as a matter of course. But, then shouldn't the suspicion that younger people have, that fen of color have, the suspicion of a doubling down on strategies that demonstrably don't work, be understandable as well? And if we're tired, shouldn't we be happy for the help?

It reminds me of this. My daughter and her partner bought a new house last year. My husband and I are planning on downsizing. Next year we likely won't have room to host the family Thanksgiving and Christmas. Wendy now has the room and offered to host the parties. This is a good thing. I want this. The next generation needs to take this over before my knees finally give out.

I was surprised, however, when I got kicked out of her kitchen three times on Thanksgiving. That's just counting the times she told me to get out. There were the other times she just stood in the pathway bouncing Baby Danny on her hip. For some reason she wanted to be in charge. In her own kitchen. When she called me to finalize Christmas plans and found me in tears because I wasn't hosting it, she suggested we go ahead and have it at my house one last time. I want this transition, but it is so very difficult. Intellectually I know it is not a rejection. Intellectually this is something I've been preparing for since my children were born.

I can't help but think that this is part of what the founders of WisCon are going through. They have built a thing. An important thing. For Jeanne Gomoll in particular this has been her life's work. And the transition feels like rejection. It hurts. For all the planning, for all the Big Book of Jobs that was supposed to pass on institutional knowledge, at some point the kids have to kick us out of the kitchen and make the event their own.

That in itself is difficult enough, as far as it goes. But, WisCon has always been more than just an sf convention. The secret life of WisCon has also always been about using art and culture to change the world. And it was the failure to come to agreement about how to achieve this that led to the WisCon coup.

Over the summer of 2014 the WisCon ConCom suffered through a major leadership shift. This was understandably made more difficult by the fact that the original ConCom insisted that they didn't have any leadership, that they were governed by a form of feminist consensus that treated every voice equally. In order to understand how that particular form of consensus failed, we need a little history to explain how WisCon evolved using both the best and the worst tendencies of white feminism but failed to adapt to intersectionality.

WisCon was born as the "world's only feminist science fiction convention" when Jeanne Gomoll and Janice Bogstad and Lesleigh Lutrell wanted something more than being auxiliaried/sidelined in fandom. Many of us feminists of a certain age found sf through the work of the giants of the New Wave, writers of the 1970s Joanna Russ, James Tiptree, Jr., Pamela Sargent, Vonda McIntyre, Zena Henderson. Naturally, Jeanne and Jan wanted to talk about them in the same way the guys talked about the "good old days" of the "golden age of science fiction."

According to the oft told tale in WisCon lore, at Worldcon 34|MidAmericon 1, the literary critic and sf fan Susan Wood proposed a women in science fiction panel. Wood describes it herself in the WisCon 20 Souvenir Book, "September 1976. The panel I proposed and planned 'Women in Science Fiction' for MidAmericon is organized. I spent three months writing to women, asking for participation and suggestions… Letters, letters, and problems with some of the MAC people, the least of which is the fact they want to cancel the panel, or run the dirty-jokes panel 'to give the men equal time'… I insist on—and get—the right to use a smaller room for two hours as a discussion room, after the 1½ hour formal panel."[3]

Worldcon programming thought there would be little interest and tucked the panel out of the way in a tiny room. What happened next convinced Jeanne that not only was there interest in women in sf, there was enough interest for a whole convention. "As it turned out, there was a rather huge number of people interested in it, and the 100 or so folks who had managed to squeeze into the room, or who had stood around outside the room trying to hear what was being said inside, stuck around in the lounge outside the panel room for several hours afterwards, talking with one another and networking… And Jeanne and Jan began to talk about a convention where there would be more than a single 'women and sf' panel."[4]

⚬

I have a confession to make. I don't really know if I'm a member of fandom or not. I have such a long, uncomfortable relationship with the little corner I've claimed as my own. WisCon is the only con I've ever been to. I go to panels, I've even been on panels where

3 Susan Wood, "People's Programming," *WisCon 20 Souvenir Book*, 1996.

4 http://blog.wiscon.info/2015/09/40x40-wiscon-1/.

I've had the opportunity to speak frankly about the issues that have marginalized me. Where I haven't had to pretend to be someone I'm not because it makes other people uncomfortable, where I've heard people imagine a world where things can be different.

Well, here's a science reference for you. The difference between mechanical sciences and biological sciences is that mechanical sciences are predictable. Experiments in the mechanical sciences can be recreated. If you set up the same inputs you will get the same results. Mechanical experiments take place within closed systems.

The biological and social sciences happen within open systems. While closed systems always have a predictable end state, in biological systems change is unpredictable. It happens at the edge of chaos.[5] I'm drawn to that edge. Fandom has never felt inclusive to me. It's felt like another hierarchy, a mechanical system designed to obfuscate and minimize chaos, a reactive often oppressive system, that has somewhere lost within it the power to reinvent the future.

Here's a metaphor. Society builds hierarchies, and hierarchies are nothing if not adaptable. We wanted to destroy the patriarchy, but as much as we tried, as much

5 "Closed systems always have a predictable end state. Although they might do unpredictable things along the way, they always, eventually, head toward maximum entropy equilibrium. Open systems are much more complicated. Sometimes they can be in a stable, equilibrium-like state, or they can exhibit very complex and unpredictable behavior patterns that are far from equilibrium—patterns such as exponential growth, radical collapse, or oscillations. As long as an open system has free energy, it may be impossible to predict its ultimate end state or whether it will ever reach an end state." Eric D. Beinhocker, *The Origin of Wealth*, Harvard Business School Press, 2006, 2007, p. 69.

as we practiced consensus, as much as we desired to be inclusive, we kept recreating hierarchies. White feminist theory became subsumed into the social studies departments of academe. WisCon developed hidden hierarchies to protect its feminism from larger fandom, and new secret masters of fandom were developed.

I'd heard about WisCon for years before I attended one; I'm a Madison local after all. I remember when Joan D. Vinge was guest of honor. Vinge's *The Snow Queen* was one of those books you hang on to, those books where things are bleak but get better when the thing we can't yet imagine becomes true. I didn't go to that WisCon. It just wasn't the kind of thing I would ever do. I was a welfare mom. I knew how the world looked at me if I bought one of my kids a candy bar. Go to an sf convention for fun? Not likely.

The first WisCon I attended was WisCon 20. Ursula Le Guin was GOH, and Judith Merril was a special guest. It was a who's who of people I'd read and loved for years. I didn't know the etiquette of interacting at cons and was able to corner Nancy Kress in the bathroom and tell her how much I'd loved "Margin of Error." She didn't seem to mind. I wandered in and out of panels, parties, and the con suite, but all the largely local attendees seemed to keep to themselves, high school cliques all over again and me without the secret handshake. It was amazing, and I had a good time, but I didn't find my "tribe."

A few weeks after the con I got a post card in the mail— "If you want to save WisCon come to Union South on such and such a date." I went, and that's how I became a member of the ConCom. I found out at that meeting that putting together 20 had tapped about all of the resources that the current ConCom had, and they weren't even sure if they could pull off 21. They were looking for new blood.

ConCom meetings in the late nineties and early aughts were held in Jim Hudson's home. They had the air of a party where I didn't know anyone. Discussions were often continuations of things that were being discussed at the regular book club meetings or in the APA[6] to which many of the members belonged. Committee reports consisted of announcements that "everything was under control."

Discussions about the upcoming convention itself followed a modified consensus[7] format. Technically, anyone who showed up for ConCom meetings was a member of the ConCom and had an equal voice in decision-making. Technically, anyone who volunteered for a position could decide how that position would be run within the ConCom. At the same time, there was a hidden hierarchy where much of the decision-making happened.

The programming committee was particularly secretive. Over the years from WisCon 20 to 30, programming was led or influenced by Jeanne Gomoll, Debbie Notkin, and/or Jane Hawkins, and they controlled the ultimate decision-making. The public process was that *anyone* could submit a programming item and *anyone* could volunteer to be on programming. These were the days when the final program was put together manually using white boards and cards and many many volunteer hours on the part of the programming team. Members

6 Amateur Press Association—individual printed articles are sent and produced by a central, usually rotating, mailer for collation and distribution.

7 Consensus—The whiners always win.

of that team were chosen by a secret cabal, or at least that's how it seemed to me. I tried to volunteer numerous times but never made the cut. The rationale was that it was a difficult, manual process, too difficult to bring in anyone new.

The goal was to have socially conscious programming, and I'm sure that the secrecy was greatly influenced by the difficulty in putting together women in sf panels at other conventions (see Susan Wood's comments above). Decades before social media activism and internet trolling, it was common at WisCon to find trolls of another sort. People who sat in the audience or volunteered for panels for the sole purpose of presenting ad hominin attacks.

What became increasingly clear at the official ConCom meetings was that 20 had been a coup in its own right. The list of former guests of honor partially tells the tale. Guests who were clearly feminist sf luminaries such as Susan Wood (WisCon 2), Suzy McKee Charnas (3), Octavia Butler (4), Suzette Haden Elgin (6), and Samuel Delany (11) were interspersed with the more usual suspects for sf GOHs David Hartwell (4), Connie Willis (11), George R. R. Martin (12), and James Frenkel (18).

Planning for 20 actually began two years prior to the convention, with the core group pulling out of other ConCom business for both 18 and 19. Jeanne Gomoll coordinated that year; programming was run by Steve Swartz. Database programming for programming was run by Jane Hawkins. Other notable members of the ConCom were Scott Custis, Emma Humphries, Hope Keifer, Karen Babich, and Jim Hudson. Not all of these were locals. The non-locals didn't attend the in-person meetings, and at that time there were no call-in meetings.

I remain curious about what happened between 15 and 20. The ConCom founders who were active after 20 were very circumspect about the shift. They were still friends with the Madison regulars who just wanted an "apolitical" (read non-feminist) convention. For an insider/outsider like me it was impossible to tell who other than Jeanne Gomoll, Scott Custis, Debbie Notkin, Diane Martin, and Jim Hudson was involved in planning from a commitment to feminism and who was involved in WisCon because it was the local con. So, although on the one hand we operated under consensus at the ConCom meetings, most of the crucial decision-making that made WisCon a feminist con happened in a space inaccessible to newer ConCom members and under a hierarchy with feminist founding members at the apex.

Key to white feminism was the consciousness-raising session. These meetings were organized to encourage women to articulate the personal and political issues that were important to us. The process was just as important as the content. We were searching for ways to understand how personal oppressions were caused by political systems, to find the very vocabulary we needed to talk about women's oppression, and to work together in ways that were in direct opposition to the patriarchal structures that oppressed us.

We encouraged women who felt silenced to speak out and discouraged any single woman from taking over the discussion by using a bowl of stones. We would sit together in a circle with the bowl of stones in the center. We would each take a single stone. If we had something to say we threw the stone back in after we spoke. You didn't have another chance to speak until no one was left holding a stone. Only when all the stones were back in the bowl could they be drawn again for a second chance to speak. The meetings had organizers, but no leaders.

Like many of us, I entered politics as a Vietnam War protester. Almost all of the consciousness-raising sessions I attended were meetings held within larger days of protest that were focused on anti-war activities. The issues discussed in the consciousness-raising groups were about the subordinate position women held in anti-war organizations and in their personal relationships that echoed the former.

I remember in particular one rally I attended in Madison in 1971. When joining the queue to enter the room set aside for feminist discussion, I noticed another woman who was being shadowed by her boyfriend and seemed somewhat reluctant to enter. When she finally made up her mind, her boyfriend followed her in. He was asked to wait outside by the organizer, and the rest of us were asked to decide on whether this session would allow men to attend. There was some discussion followed by a show of hands. Some people okayed him, some didn't raise their hand, and one person voted that we should have a woman-only meeting. He was not allowed in.

This was an extremely powerful moment for me. I had been raised with majority rules. The idea that if even one person might be potentially silenced we would not allow this young man to take part was life changing. The idea that power relationships mattered, that the needs of the marginalized could be privileged, totally changed my thinking about social justice movements. It was this type of experience in feminism that led to Jeanne's unwavering support for dedicated space (later called safer space) for POC at WisCon.

Early consciousness-raising groups strove to design more democratic operating procedures in opposition to other forms of structured, hierarchical organizing principals, but were prone to what Jo Freeman called the tyranny of structurelessness.[8] This antidote to hierarchy came with its own set of problems, the chief of which was the inevitable formation of informal, unacknowledged power elites within the organizations. "Thus structurelessness becomes a way of masking power, and within the women's movement is usually most strongly advocated by those who are the most powerful (whether they are conscious of their power or not). As long as the structure of the group is informal, the rules of how decisions are made are known only to a few, and awareness of power is limited to those who know the rules. Those who do not know the rules and are not chosen for initiation must remain in confusion, or suffer from paranoid delusions that something is happening of which they are not quite aware."[9]

The most egregious results for the women's movement of these informal power structures was the inability of white feminists to acknowledge the harm they did to feminists of color by requiring a narrow definition of feminism, causing a schism along intersectional fault lines. The other no less damaging result was the insistence of certain leaders of the white feminist movement that they alone could determine who was and wasn't a woman and, in the name of protecting women, damage transwomen, an already dangerously marginalized group of women. The results of all of the above are painfully obvious to

8 Jo Freeman, "The Tyranny of Structurelessness," JoFreeman.com, http://www.jofreeman.com/joreen/tyranny.htm.

9 Ibid.

the younger generation of feminists who by 2014 had no more fucks to give for the founders of white feminism.

The informal power rules delineated above operated in WisCon as well. As new members joined the ConCom, particularly after the large conventions of 20 and 30, it was clear that decisions were being made outside of official communications channels and scheduled meetings. It made newer ConCom members feel like second-tier members. Lack of transparency was a frequent and common complaint. It could feel like being at the convention itself and always wondering where the secret parties were going on. Over the years many people left the ConCom because of this.

I volunteered to be GOH liaison for Sheri Tepper when the topic of volunteering came up pre-22 and it was announced that that position was open. People thanked me for volunteering, and I thought it was settled. At the next meeting, it was announced that actually Tepper's liaison would be someone else, someone with a longer track record with WisCon than me. I never could figure out what the procedures were for volunteering, which positions were really open and which were only open if one of the core members didn't want it. The existing power structures proved difficult to explain. The core group of WisCon founders who benefitted from these informal power structures did not possess the feminist analysis of group structure pointed out by Jo Freeman.

I only found Freeman's work myself while undertaking research for this essay and looking for explanations in feminist theory for how a group that had all the right intentions could so miserably fail at setting up a process that would not privilege older white members. I was also looking for something to explain why, no matter how hard I had worked on the ConCom from 21 to 29, I never became more than an insider/outsider.

Never having heard of Freeman is a result of the process of the media creating celebrity feminists and consigning others to the dustbin of history, so to speak. The media platforms available to seventies feminists, television, radio, and magazines, privileged white feminists such as Betty Friedan and Gloria Steinem whose messages reinforced capitalist patriarchy and only asked that women have access to the same careers and salaries available to men. Freeman's work was published in feminist newsletters for specific organizations and not widely disseminated. Ironically, feminists who were not active in the right circles would never have been exposed to it.

I edited the Souvenir Book with little help or feedback from 21 through 29. When planning for 30 rolled around, Jeanne decided that she wanted a different type of Souvenir Book for the anniversary con. I was informed that someone else would be producing it for 30 and dismissed from the job. Again, I experienced having a job that I had volunteered for taken away and assigned to someone else without discussion or fanfare. Not to be whiney, but this was so in opposition to how I had been told the ConCom operated that I was left wondering what *I* had done that was obviously inadequate.

When I joined the ConCom in 1996, power was organized informally among a network of friends who had worked together for twenty years. At the time of the WisCon coup in 2014, this informal power structure had been in existence for thirty-eight years. Calls for greater transparency could never reveal the bones of this entrenched and unacknowledged power structure. Without feminist theory, calls for transparency resulted in documenting and organizing tasks, the "big book of jobs" for example.

If asked, the pre-coup ConCom would say that the ConCom operated under a form of feminist consensus, an unstructured form of consensus that was considered to be de facto feminist. There was no perceived need to discuss what was meant by the feminist organizing principals of WisCon. So, at times the ConCom seemed to operate along the lines of structureless consciousness-raising groups while totally forgetting any methodology designed to equalize power toward the powerless. At times it seemed to operate at the level of modified consensus where all voices mattered equally, falling into the trap of giving Richard Russell a platform for objecting to the POC safer space ad nauseum, long after the issue had been fought and won.

Consensus itself as a formal organizing tool did not become widely accepted until 1976 when the Clamshell Alliance adopted it as an organizing tool in planning their direct action against the Seabrook Nuclear Plant.[10] They adopted the process from the Quakers and formalized the practice. The process was similar enough to early feminist consciousness-raising groups to make sense as a next step in addressing the problems of structurelessness, including the inability of consciousness-raising groups to go beyond exercises in personal examination and empowerment to engage in direct action.

The economist Yves Smith[11] does a good job of detailing the problems inherent in consensus. "In practice,

10 Yves Smith, "Why the Consensus Process has a Poor Track Record in Activist Movements," *naked capitalism*, June 9, 2015, http://www.nakedcapitalism.com/2015/06/why-the-consensus-process-has-a-poor-track-record-in-activist-movements.html.

11 Do you get the joke in her name? It took me *ages*.

the process often worked well in small-group settings, including within the affinity groups that often formed the building blocks for large actions. At the scale of a significant mobilization, though, the process was fraught with difficulty from the start… Movement after movement found, moreover, that the process tended to give great attention and weight to the concerns of a few dissenters. In the purest form of consensus, a block by one or two individuals could bring the whole group to a screeching halt…it also consistently empowered cranks, malcontents, and even provocateurs to lay claim to a group's attention and gum up the works"[12]

Within feminism, first the unstructured nature of consciousness-raising groups and later consensus problem-solving became definitionally accepted as feminist organizing principals. My generation of feminists could no longer even raise reasonable arguments to defend them, but were willing to brand any opposition to these organizing structures as anti-feminist, regardless of the fact that they did not meet the needs of WOC and other multiply marginalized groups.

My personal experience of the ConCom encompasses the time I became active just prior to 21, through 29 (when I was asked to step back), on through the coup when my involvement with preconvention activities had significantly dwindled. When certain events are looked at in a framework of feminist activism, patterns emerge.

So, here's another thing. For a time the fantasy writer N. K. Jemisin ran the WisCon Writer's Workshop. She started doing this before the sale of her first novel. She attended ConCom meetings over the conference phone.

12 Ibid.

She was in attendance the year that Elizabeth Moon was slated to be GOH. That would have been 35 in 2011.

If you don't remember, on September 11, 2010, Ms Moon wrote a blog post on Islam that had the potential to fuel and was fueled by a significant American anti-Muslim sentiment. The short- and long-term responses to this by the WisCon ConCom made apparent the gulf in processing intersectional feminism between white and POC feminists, between WisCon leadership and membership, and between those active in social media and those largely unaware of social media conversations.

The question before the ConCom was— Do we disinvite Elizabeth Moon for taking an action that is sure to make Muslim members of the convention feel unwelcome? I won't go through the history of that event here; most of the discussion is still available online. I'll tell you why I brought up Nora (N. K. Jemisin) in this context. At one point during a ConCom discussion of what to do, Nora remarked, "Isn't the convention supposed to be fun?" meaning of course how can it be fun if the needs of large potential groups of members are considered less important.

For me, WisCon has never been about having fun. It's always been about changing the world. I had opinions about disinviting Moon, but I wasn't qualified to make them known. I am not marginalized on the axis of color. I don't have the lived experience to tell POC what sacrifices they need to make for the good of the convention. I believe in the end the ConCom made the right call under pressure.

WisCon stopped being fun for Nora. She quit the ConCom.[13] A few years after WisCon disinvited Moon,

13 N. K. Jemisin, "WisCon: I'm Done," October 18, 2010, http://nojojojo.livejournal.com/223115.html.

Nora became the center of an uninvited fandom shit-storm. She had the temerity to call for reconciliation in her GOH speech at Continuum IX, Australia's 2013 Speculative Fiction Convention. Part of her speech was a response to the chainmail bikini-gate and SFWA Bulletin editorship "kerfuffles" referenced earlier in this essay.[14] What she discovered was that this was a war. "For those of you who don't stay on top of the latest news in the genre, let me recap what happened after that speech: I was textually assaulted by a bigot who decided to call me a 'half-savage' among other things… He did this via the Science Fiction and Fantasy Writers of America's official Twitter feed."[15] As a black woman fantasy writer, Nora doesn't get to choose fun.

The white ConCom misunderstood what the problem was about. The white ConCom had become more professional over the years and defaulted to rules of event organization that individuals had learned in a professional context. Whether or not to disinvite Moon was approached within a framework of what was best for the reputation of the convention.

Some ConCom members believed that the issues of inclusion and access being discussed in the larger sf world were separate issues. Without theory it is impossible to devise truly egalitarian organizational structures. It is similar to the time years ago when I tried to introduce inclusivity tools to the meeting format of the Democratic Socialists of America. As my young, white,

---

14 N. K. Jemisin, "Guest of Honor Speech for Continuum IX," *Systems Fail*, Hiromi Goto and N. K. Jemisin, Aqueduct Press, Seattle, WA, 2014.

15 N. K. Jemisin, "WisCon 38 Guest of Honor Speech," *The WisCon Chronicles Vol. 9, ed.* Mary Anne Mohanraj, Aqueduct Press, Seattle WA, 2015.

male, pre-law student colleague told me, "Too complicated. Let's just use Robert's Rules of Order. They've always worked for me."

WisCon does not just happen in the meeting rooms of the Concourse hotel on Memorial Day weekend. WisCon is not owned by the ConCom or even by SF3. In most ways the members make it happen, and the members have a significant emotional investment in the kind of feminism that happens at WisCon. It took a social media campaign to convince the ConCom that the question of what to do about Elizabeth Moon was a question of voice and safety for fen of color. This was not the last time the ConCom made this mistake.

A core group of WisCon had fought for years in the context of a consensus-driven organization to make WisCon an inclusive feminist convention. As far back as September of 2003, the ConCom held a facilitated retreat in Madison. The purpose of the retreat was two-fold: how to safeguard institutional memory and how to make sure that WisCon's mission as a feminist convention would continue.

Since I don't do other conventions, I was able to meet ConCom members who had been active on committees but did not usually attend the ConCom meetings. I met Carrie Ferguson, Karen Babich, and Betsey Lundsten, who are still active on the post-coup ConCom. The only person of color at the retreat to my knowledge was Victor Raymond.[16]

---

16 My report on the retreat comes from my own arguably limited memories, conversations with Daniel Dexter shortly after the retreat and again before writing this article, and extensive notes compiled by Diane Martin during the retreat and distributed to all of the attendees the following May (special

Jeanne, Scott, Diane, and Jim had two meetings with the facilitator prior to the retreat and came up with four topics for discussion: Feminism and Focus, Organizational Challenges, Special Treatment, and Does Size Matter. People were randomly assigned working groups. I missed the topic breakdown as I had to work that morning, but arrived in time for each of the groups to report back to the whole and to take part in the discussion of topics within the larger group.

Some of the discussion on Feminism and Focus had to do with a complaint that had been made to the ConCom earlier that year. Two thousand and three was a presidential primary year. George W. Bush was running for a second term. An argument could be made that with the help of his brother he had stolen the first term. Feelings were running high. Richard Russell wore a prominent vote Democrat button at the reg desk. Political discussions with an emphasis on getting out the Democratic vote were rampant on panels and in the halls. The socialist writer China Miéville was GOH.

The person who complained identified as a Republican and a feminist. She was a member of Broad Universe. She attended WisCon as her first convention and complained to the ConCom about the lack of inclusiveness. If we were a feminist convention, didn't we have an obligation to be inclusive of all feminists?

Oh, "inclusiveness," that bugbear of a word of white feminism. We cannot talk about inclusiveness without centering whiteness. We cannot talk about inclusiveness without graciously welcoming the marginalized (who by definition can't be us) to come to our party. We cannot talk about inclusiveness without being blinkered to

thanks to Dan Dexter for saving *everything*. My copy of these notes is long gone).

the true goals, interests, and desires of POC and other marginalized members of fandom. Those who do the including choose who is and isn't included.

Jeanne and I argued that feminism had to be intersectional, that a feminism that continued to marginalize members on axes of race and class was not feminism. I believe that most of those who opposed us were driven more by the feeling that WisCon had been called out and found wanting than by ideology. Squeaky-wheel thinking. But, this has been one of the traditional failures of the ConCom, a fear of being found out doing the wrong thing, with no framework to determine what that wrong thing is or what the right thing would have been. We debated feminist focus in 2003, but never came to an agreement.

And then there was Richard. Richard argued that we were a science fiction convention first that focused on feminism. The inability to see how these ideas were intertwined in the concept feminist science fiction was an early precursor of the way he remained blinkered in understanding what intersectionality meant to the convention. At the retreat Richard opined that we shouldn't go overboard on feminism and abandon sf. That if we had to choose between Jerry Pournelle and Gloria Steinem as GOH we'd pick Pournelle. Luckily we never were required to pick either. Diane pointed out in her notes that this comment was received with much laughter. She doesn't make a distinction between hearty laughter and uncomfortable laughter. Oh well.

I think it was these recurring genteel fights over feminism and inclusion that led to so much of the outreach to marginalized people being done off the books, so to speak. It was so hard to tell exactly where everyone stood. Who was in agreement, who was uncertain, who was just following the path of least resistance, and why oh why did Jeanne and Scott and Jim and Diane keep protecting Richard? Only part of it was friendship. Part of it was the belief from white feminism that the way to protect marginalized voices was to protect everyone's voice.

The section on special treatment was not as awful as it sounds, although predictable problems surfaced. Most of the discussion focused on the writer's workshop. Since the founding of the writer's workshop, it had been structured with not only the clarion style peer workshops which occur today, but with opportunities for those who took part to do additional networking with each other, authors, and editors.

There were program items set up in the smaller sixth floor rooms called living rooms. These were more informal than traditional panels and gave workshop participants additional access to GOHs. You had to sign up for the living rooms in advance, and workshop participants were allowed early signup. Given fire-code restrictions in these smaller rooms, general congoers were never able to gain access.

The issue of the fairness of allowing one particular group this kind of access and denying it to general membership was a contentious one. Terri Windling 23 GOH was particularly appalled and refused to take part. The living rooms were eventually dropped.

The elitism of the Governor's Club was also discussed. Richard made a passing comment that affirmative action drives a lot of special treatment. There were calls for more transparency in how we decided to use and prioritize limited resources. The safer space for POC was not discussed.

A result of the retreat was the first attempt at crafting a mission statement. This statement was updated as a Statement of Principals after the Elizabeth Moon episode and again after the coup. The Big Book of Jobs was started as a way to capture institutional memory. The structure of having department leads and apprentices was put into place.

Recruitment of marginalized people to membership and the ConCom went back underground. But slowly POC became more involved in WisCon. WisCon became more welcoming to queer and disabled people. Anonymous grants appeared that allowed the attendance and participation of marginalized people.

WisCon had always been inclined to invite and celebrate writers at the beginnings of their careers. I met Nalo Hopkinson, 26 GOH, at my first WisCon 20 in 1996. *Brown Girl in the Ring* came out in 1998. When she was honored at 26, her bibliography consisted of short fiction, two novels, *Brown Girl in the Ring* and *Midnight Robber*, and *Whispers from the Cotton Tree Root*, an anthology she edited.

The POC safer space, an issue since 1999, was finally instituted in 2009 for WisCon 33. WisCon 34 honored both Mary Anne Mohanraj and Nnedi Okorafor. There was an increased presence of POC new to fandom, who came specifically to see Mohanraj and Okorafor. This was a turning point for the convention in which white-centered inclusion and the insider rules of sf fandom were no longer enough. New members brought an analysis of the power of fiction to change the world that many white feminists were afraid to speak out loud.

The incrementalist approach of backroom deals was no longer enough. Incrementalism of course can never work. Systems are nothing if not adaptive, including systems of oppression. Complexity Theory as applied to systems theory offers a better analysis of how change happens. Complexity scientists suggest that living systems migrate to a state of dynamic stability they call "the edge of chaos." Mitchell Waldrop provides a description of the edge of chaos in his book, *Complexity*:

> The balance point—often called the edge of chaos—is where the components of a system never quite lock into place, and yet never quite dissolve into turbulence either… The edge of chaos is where new ideas and innovative genotypes are forever nibbling away at the edges of the status quo, and where even the most entrenched old guard will eventually be overthrown. The edge of chaos is where centuries of slavery and segregation suddenly give way to the civil rights movement of the 1950s and 1960s; where seventy years of Soviet communism suddenly give way to political turmoil and ferment; where eons of evolutionary stability suddenly give way to wholesale species transformation.[17]

The idea of progressive incrementalism is so firmly implanted in white liberal minds that direct evidence cannot dislodge it. I was on a panel years ago with the late, great linguist Suzette Haden Elgin (WisCon 6 GOH). She was talking about the intractable problems that women in her beloved Ozarks were faced with. It was a depressing conversation. A hand went up in the audience, "Ms Elgin, are you saying that things aren't getting better?"

---

17 Mitchell Waldrop, *Complexity*, cited in John Cleveland, "Complexity Theory, Basic Concepts and application to Systems Thinking, Innovation Network for Communities," Mar. 27, 1994.

"No." She paused for effect. "I'm saying that things are getting worse."

This is the incomprehension that POC face when they try to explain their lived experience to white folks. This is the incomprehension that resulted in Richard Russell being allowed to argue against the POC safer space at ConCom meeting after meeting using anti-segregation arguments that contained accusations of reverse racism.

Change happens at the edge of chaos. The summer of 2014 was the edge of chaos for WisCon.

⊸

The WisCon ConCom itself is a subcommittee of the Society for the Furtherance & Study of Fantasy & Science Fiction. SF3 began as a group of local fans who got together to form a book club and to discuss science fiction. WisCon was set up as a subcommittee of SF3, with the chair of WisCon being voted in by the board. There was little official direction from SF3 in the running of the Con; however, when controversial ConCom matters needed to be resolved, they were referred back to SF3, the governing body. Oftentimes this would be the first time many ConCom members had even heard of SF3. While part of the role of SF3 was to protect the Con Chairs who change every year, to the wider membership it seemed that SF3 was a secret organization that only protected its friends.

Neither the ConCom nor SF3 are monoliths. I've detailed some of the internal conflicts above. As younger people and people from marginalized communities were increasingly recruited to membership and service on the ConCom, the lack of accountability inherent in consensus organizations led to a feeling that there must be a conspiracy protecting the parties that were causing harm to particular communities.

After the Elizabeth Moon and James Frenkel incidents, the membership took to twitter, and the speed and breadth of these conversations of dissatisfaction increased. In every instance the ConCom seemed to waver in its stance, when it was actually the unwieldiness of a volunteer organization run by consensus. Every decision took time. Every decision was argued from every angle. For marginalized members and ConCom volunteers it appeared they were frequently called upon to bring older white feminists up to speed on social justice issues with white feminists (whose intentions were good) demanding to remain unaccountable for problems that they caused.

Elizabeth Moon was disinvited as GOH by the chair of SF3, Jeanne Gomoll at the time. Jim Frenkel, after much delay was partially banned from the convention, with a path to redemption built into the announcement; he would have recourse. The membership felt betrayed. The way harassment was handled at sf conventions, professional conferences in the tech industry, and in the skeptic community, three communities with much crossover, had been changing.

Systems operating near the edge of chaos are involved in the struggle to protect the status quo on one side and to institute substantive change on the other. This change is neither automatic nor progressive. Eventually a tipping point is reached where the status quo begins to change. This is never one single event, but the result of a preponderance of events that combine to change the accepted narrative and to increasingly empower those on the side of change. WisCon at its feminist best worked toward empowerment over inclusion.

In the matter of fandom, the tipping point over harassment had been building. The status quo that protected harassers and required victims to shrug it off or leave the community was no longer acceptable. As incident after incident became public and was poorly handled, members' demand for change increased.

There were two major issues with the way the Frenkel incident was handled. The precedent in fandom had been to treat each incident as separate and to give the perpetrator the benefit of the doubt and/or opportunity for redemption. The other problem was simply a lack of follow-through inherent in the way volunteer organizations with annual leadership changes work.

Although the initial report seemed to have been handled well, after the convention the safety committee changed, conchairs changed, and the ConCom went on summer hiatus. There were no systems in place to carry through with follow-up from year to year. Frenkel's involvement in 38 was a shock to everyone on the ConCom. Department chairs asked for an official ruling on his involvement in programming. His offer to volunteer at the consuite, historically understaffed, was accepted when no one objected.

WisCon appeared to be dragging its feet, and the membership at large wondered if this was a result of the ConCom's upholding the status quo. The further removed people were who engaged in the twitter, LiveJournal, and Tumblr conversations, the more personal the attacks against ConCom leadership became.

When Debbie Notkin, who originally chaired the Frenkel harassment subcommittee, was accused of protecting Frenkel, she resigned from the committee and publicly apologized for the mistakes she made. She specifically apologized for not bringing in Frenkel's history of abuse in other venues and not passing that information on to the rest of the committee. She had made her best attempt to be fair in a difficult situation. It is my belief that she relied on an outmoded idea of fairness that more closely resembled a legal/professional analysis, allowing benefit of the doubt to the accused while failing to protect the interests of other con members. It was an extremely painful lesson in the changing landscape of intersectional feminism.

For the first time, an issue confronting the ConCom was brought to a vote. Motions were made, and an email vote of all members of the ConCom was called. This meant a decision had to be made on who comprised the ConCom. When I was most active on the ConCom from 21 to 30, anyone who wanted to be on the ConCom and came to meetings was considered a ConCom member. This was never a formal rule.

As the ConCom became bigger and meetings became more professionally run, only those members who headed departments attended the meetings. The ConCom Google group was another matter. Virtually anyone who wanted to volunteer for the convention was eligible to join the Google Group, and everyone had a stake in the Frenkel decision. Were members of the Google group ConCom members? Under the original, unexplained definition they absolutely were, if they wanted to be. It was decided that anyone who had been actively involved in any of the last two conventions was eligible to vote. The ConCom voted for a lifetime ban.

As difficult as going through all of this was, it wasn't the Frenkel incident that broke the ConCom. As this was going on, a number of long-time ConCom members, most vocally Richard Russell, came out in defense of Frenkel. Relying on years of personal relationships, they denied the possibility that he could have harassed anyone. At best they posited that Matthesen simply misunderstood.

In order to finally put a stop to the "empowered cranks and malcontents" problem of consensus organizations, a segment of the ConCom membership took a pragmatic approach. They first staged a coup of SF3.

For the first time a large number of ConCom members joined SF3 and ran for board positions. A rule that motions could be proposed and voted on via phone attendance resulted in non-Madison locals being able to amass the numbers to make a change.

This was a move brilliant in its simplicity. For decades SF3 leadership had been asking ConCom members to become more involved in SF3. There were a couple of years when my partner and I joined to strengthen the numbers supporting the POC safer space. We were repeatedly told that would be an issue decided by the next convention committee. Again, it was never clear where final decision-making authority and accountability lay.

A motion was passed at the 2014 SF3 annual meeting that required ConCom members to abide by the Statement of Principals updated in the aftermath of the Frenkel decision.[18] The new board chair, Jackie Lee, sent Richard a letter removing him from the ConCom, but not banning him from the convention. "We believe that Richard's behavior is not in keeping with WisCon's Statement of Principles, which the SF3 membership has now affirmed as a policy the SF3 board and WisCon ConCom members should adhere to."[19]

They took a further step. In order to prevent future Richards, many ConCom members wanted to make sure

18 The full text of the Statement of Principles can be found here: http://account.wiscon.net/principles.php.

19 The full text of the letter was provided by Richard to Mike Glyer of File770 and is available here: http://file770.com/?p=19463.

that all WisCon members signed an agreement to abide by the Statement of Principles. To a younger generation who had come of age signing terms of service agreements for anything and everything they wanted to do online, this did not seem like a big ask. For an older generation, many of whom were one degree of separation away from people who lost their creative careers over McCarthy-era pledges, the fear that this could and would be used against them at some point was not necessarily paranoid. This proved to be the real generational barrier.

There was no official announcement of the turnover after these events. WisCon's LiveJournal reported that "the WisCon ConCom had close to a dozen people resign in the aftermath of the Frenkel harassment ban."[20] This was later clarified to "The vast majority of people left as a result of the arduous process of rewriting our harassment policy when we discovered it was severely flawed. This process took an extraordinary level of effort on the part of many members of the ConCom, well in excess of the normal amount of work involved in simply putting on the convention, and several people left as a result of the months-long discussions that happened well in advance of the ban."[21]

It should be noted that many many volunteers remained on the ConCom and in other volunteer positions. A number of long-time attendees, who have been active in increasing diversity in books, games, and fandom, took on leadership roles. WisCon 39 and 40 happened, and there is no reason to believe as I write this in 2016 that WisCon won't continue.

20 Jam, "What I Did This Summer," WisCon blog, Oct. 17, 2014: http://wiscon.livejournal.com/422325.html.

21 Ibid.

So, I had an ending in mind for this piece. I was going to wrap it back to the analogy of my daughter's kitchen last Thanksgiving and say that it was time for my generation to get out of the way, because circumstances have changed, because the contexts in which marginalized people live have come to the forefront. But...

I'm in awe of the work being done by writers of color to change the industry and change the narrative by which we all see ourselves. But, oppression is an adaptive system. I understand the need to have a safer space or at least a recuperative space, and I hope WisCon continues to fill that role. But, creating it with rules worries me.

I was going to say something, something about getting over hurt feelings and passing on the recipe for the cranberry bread already, but I'm worried that rule-based solutions to the problems that plagued the ConCom before will not address future problems. WisCon needs a theory of intersectional feminism under which to operate. I don't trust white feminists to come up with that theory. We weren't good at it. But, it needs to be done.

Oppression is adaptive. I told you my story of empowerment when my early consciousness-raising groups privileged the marginalized. But, someone decided there needed to be rules and someone to enforce the rules, and then people decided that someone else could tell women who did and did not qualify as a woman. If oppression is adaptive, justice must also be adaptive.

I don't have the answers. The only advice I can give here from my sixty-three years is this—don't stop asking the questions.

So, perhaps I will leave you with this—

> She had never feared or despised the city. It was her country. There would not be slums

like this, if the Revolution prevailed. But there would be misery. There would always be misery, waste, cruelty. She had never pretended to be changing the human condition, to be Mama taking tragedy away from the children so they won't hurt themselves. Anything but. So long as people were free to choose, if they chose to drink flybane and live in sewers, it was their business. Just so long as it wasn't the business of Business, the source of profit and the means of power for other people. She had felt all that before she knew anything; before she wrote the first pamphlet, before she left Parheo, before she knew what "capital" meant, before she'd been farther than River Street where she played roll-taggie kneeling on scabby knees on the pavement with the other six-year-olds, she had known it: that she, and the other kids, and her parents, and their parents, and the drunks and whores and all of River Street, were at the bottom of something—were the foundation, the reality, the source.[22]

22 Ursula K. Le Guin, "The Day Before the Revolution," *More Women of Wonder*, Pamela Sargent, ed., Vintage, Aug. 1976, p. 297.

About the Author

Beth Plutchak is a writer and consultant. After a twenty-year career in commercial banking she started her own business doing economic development and marketing consulting. Economics and social justice inform all of her work. She was the editor of the WisCon Souvenir Book for WisCons 21 through 29. Her essays have appeared in the Souvenir Book and in WisCon Chronicles.

Made in the USA
Lexington, KY
16 February 2017